ST ANTONY'S PAPERS · NUMBER 11
*
MIDDLE EASTERN AFFAIRS
NUMBER TWO

ST ANTONY'S PAPERS

*

ST ANTONY'S PAPERS · NUMBER 11

MIDDLE EASTERN AFFAIRS

Number Two

EDITED BY

ALBERT HOURANI

1961

Southern Illinois University Press

Carbondale, Illinois

PUBLISHED IN
GREAT BRITAIN, 1961, BY
CHATTO AND WINDUS LTD

★

PUBLISHED IN
THE UNITED STATES, 1961, BY
SOUTHERN ILLINOIS
UNIVERSITY PRESS

★

LIBRARY OF CONGRESS CATALOG
CARD NUMBER 59-7823
FIRST AMERICAN EDITION

PRINTED IN GREAT BRITAIN BY
BUTLER AND TANNER LTD
FROME AND LONDON

CONTENTS

The main emphasis of the work of St Antony's College, Oxford, since its foundation in 1950 has been in the fields of modern history and international affairs. The College organizes a number of regular Seminars at which are read papers produced by its members in the course of their research or by visiting experts from other institutions. The College further sponsors the delivery of lectures in Oxford by scholars of international reputation in their respective fields.

An appreciable volume of contribution to scholarship is thus being produced under the auspices of St Antony's, and the present series has been started in order to preserve and present a selection of this work. This series is not, however, confined to this material alone and includes contributions from other places.

Three numbers a year are issued and each number is devoted to a particular topic or a particular part of the world.

MR BEVIN'S "ARAB POLICY"

By Elizabeth Monroe

A REGIONAL EXPERT and the Foreign Secretary see the world differently. The first tends to focus on the problems of his region only in their local context, whereas any modern foreign secretary must see all foreign affairs as interlocked. In the years just after the Second World War, the so-called Arab expert was inclined to be especially parochial. For six years the pattern of the war had turned his parish into a virtual island, and, in the first four years after it, both his outlook and that of the local people with whom he was dealing grew narrower owing to the poignancy of their emotions about Palestine.

The years just mentioned were those of Mr Bevin's heyday, and throughout them British Middle Eastern policy was constantly affected —even governed—by the prime anxieties of the time, all of which lay outside the Middle East. Europe, being both nearer home and much more profoundly disrupted by the war, was bound to come first with any British statesman—whether the Foreign Secretary (Mr Bevin), the Chancellor of the Exchequer (Dr Dalton) or the President of the Board of Trade (Sir Stafford Cripps). The principal items that held their attention were the survival of the victor at the best standard of living that could be secured on an empty treasury, the struggle with the Soviet Union over the no-man's-lands in Central Europe—principally Germany—and the rebuilding of western European industry and employment as a barrier to the spread of communism.

Some of these major troubles might well have worried the inhabitants of the Middle East, but they did not. Even the one which impinged most nearly on their interests, which was the Soviet engulfment of Eastern Europe, did not do so. To Arabs, the struggle for Europe might have been happening on another planet; what mattered was the disposal of the hordes of foreign troops that were still milling round their countries although, by their standards, all danger of invasion had ended in 1943. To the Arabs of the Fertile Crescent in particular, a second subject of perpetual worry was the future of Palestine. At the time, Soviet pressure on their region was being exercised at several

points—on Turkey, on Persian Azerbaijan and, as a bargaining counter, on the Council of Foreign Ministers for a trusteeship in Libya; but
this pressure dwindled during 1946, and, except in Persia, faded out.
It therefore moved in inverse ratio to Soviet pressure in Europe and,
as it decreased, lulled the Arabs into a sense of complacency, and of
safety from all encroachments except from those of Britain.

Even the British and American citizens in the area focused their
attention on purely local matters. No doubt they would have related
their problems to Europe's if the statesmen in office at home had published their misgivings and frustrations about Soviet policy. But none
did so. The men at the top—Attlee, Bevin, Truman, Byrnes and others
—were soon aghast at Soviet sharp practice, but all withheld public
comment. They dissembled either because of their hope that relations
would improve somewhere on Russia's great periphery, or because of
the great goodwill which the Soviet Union still commanded everywhere; anyone who spoke up raised a storm of protest from people
as far apart in outlook as the Keep-Lefters in Britain and the anti-
colonialists in the United States. Mr Churchill's speech at Fulton,
Missouri, on March 5, 1946, calling for an Anglo-American alliance
against the Soviet Union was later to become a statement of the
obvious, but at the time it struck much of the world as surprising,
die-hard and exaggerated.

The Arabs, therefore, were unaware of British anxieties. By the time
these were publishable—that is, by the second half of 1947—they had
no time for such topics. Disillusioning events such as Soviet bullyings
and murders in the Balkans, Soviet refusal to let the satellite states
profit by the Marshall Plan, and Soviet creation of the Cominform,
passed them by. For in the winter of 1947/8 their attention was
riveted on the unity of the Nile Valley, the ejection of British troops
from Egypt and Iraq, and the armed struggle which had begun for
Palestine.

When Mr Bevin took over the Foreign Secretaryship in July 1945,
he brought socialist conviction to the job. Diplomacy was a talent to be
exercised on behalf of the people; British and European productivity
must be re-started as soon as possible, and living standards raised in less
developed areas as soon as possible after that; multiple security arrangements were preferable to treaties of alliance, and the stationing of
troops on foreign soil ought not to be negotiated under duress. But for

nearly half of his five-and-a-half years in office, these targets were unattainable because of the muddle in which the war had left the world. For over two years, all his major speeches refer to its prostration. In the Middle East in 1945, confusion was made worse by the need to cancel three months' arrangements for a major staging-post during a long war with Japan; suddenly, most of the troops and goods that were coursing through its corridors had to change direction as the world turned over to demobilization, collecting prisoners, mopping up Japanese-held islands, sweeping mines and feeding liberated Asia as well as liberated Europe.

The stresses of this change of gear help to account for acts of the time that were out of keeping with the new Labour cabinet's principles. One such example was its inept failure to remove the British troops in Egypt out of the inflammable political atmosphere of the Nile Valley, and into the legitimate treaty zone on the Suez Canal. This mistake is often put down to personal foibles; "they were warned of the danger of not doing it, but they took no action until much too late", later said Lord Altrincham, who had been the last of the wartime British Ministers of State in the Middle East.[1] But warnings or no warnings, one of the initial reasons for that misguided pause on the Nile was lack of the authorization and the shipping needed to produce alternative accommodation on the Canal in the quantity required.

There were some compelling reasons for leaving troops wherever they could legitimately be left in the Middle East. A Soviet drive for the insulation of southern Russia was taking the form of encouragement to the Greek communists, and of pressure on Turkey for special rights to garrison the Straits, as well as on Persia through the establishment of a puppet government in Persian Azerbaijan. Therefore a British cabinet that was as much inclined to be liberal to Egypt as to India found itself unable to treat the first as it was treating the second. To Arabs and Egyptians, this difference was not apparent; pressure on Greeks, Turks and Persians seemed to them remote and, except in the eyes of a few Iraqi elder statesmen, was not alarming. But by British reckoning, India was insulated from the Soviet Union by a glacis of mountains, uncoveted areas and unaffected territories, whereas Iraq and Egypt were not. Necessity, as well as habit and tradition, constrained the Foreign Office to press for new military agreements with the Arab states.

Treaties with some existed already. In Egypt, Iraq, Transjordan and, of course, Palestine, there were unexpired rights to station British

[1] House of Lords, May 21, 1946.

troops; by the spring of 1946, all such forces had been withdrawn from Persia, and also from Syria in step with the unwilling French. The existing Egyptian treaty was described by Mr Bevin, in a note of January 1946 answering an Egyptian request for revision, as of "essential soundness" in its "fundamental principles". Yet, as a socialist, he was sensitive to the upsurge of nationalist feeling everywhere, and to the impropriety of trying for concessions under pressure of an occupation. At the time, the whole of liberated Europe was looking to a socialist Britain for a lead, and he and his colleagues felt fitted to give it. In their optimism, they reckoned on the same sort of role in the Middle East also, encouraged to this conclusion by listening to Egyptians and others who talked about "the new spirit prevailing in the world, as witness the British election results".[2] Mr Bevin's native optimism and self-confidence, coupled with his socialist cast of mind, led him to believe that defence agreements could be negotiated with the Middle Eastern states on a new basis, and as equal partners.

But inequalities were manifest. Although a reformist Englishman might think that they could be smoothed out by goodwill and good drafting, all Egyptians and most Arabs thought otherwise. Decades of British tutelage, paternalism and offhand manners had eaten away self-confidence and generated resentment in virtually the whole of the Arab generation that grew up in the trough of the nineteen-twenties and thirties. The men who thought differently were all older, and had lived their formative years in the Ottoman Empire, which had taught them the political facts of life and given them experience of responsibility. Having learnt these facts at a time of Ottoman weakness, they also knew the value of great power connexions, and saw nothing undignified in making them. Men of the generation and stamp of King Abdullah and Nuri Pasha were ready to throw in their lot with Great Britain in a way that the paler figures of the nineteen-twenties were not; soon, both older men were written off, and later murdered, as tools of the British.

Mr Bevin, therefore, started on his round of efforts to refurbish Britain's Middle Eastern defences with many fewer bargaining counters in hand than he imagined he possessed. He needed bases, or, alternatively, re-occupation rights in the event of war. His weakness was that he had no acceptable coin to tender in return.

For the Egyptians wanted only evacuation. What is more, they felt entitled to it, both for their war services, to which many British statesmen had paid tribute, and because Syria, backed by the new

[2] Sidky Pasha, quoted in the *New York Times*, August 3, 1945.

United Nations Organization, was getting rid of foreign occupation on the grounds that troops must nowhere be stationed on the territory of a state without its consent. While awaiting satisfaction, young Egyptians had brushes with British troops—minor evidence that they could make their soil an uncomfortable base if need be.

At length, in London, the politicians and the soldiers hammered out a compromise that would fit both their requirements. Their decision was weighted on the political side, for the soldiers of the day were well accustomed to hanging on to bases in the teeth of local unpopularity, and would have been ready to organize security in the Canal Zone however hostile the Egyptian nationalists. On May 7, 1946, the British government offered to withdraw from Egypt altogether at dates to be settled by negotiation, subject to an alliance that left room for mutual military arrangements in the event of war. Yet the Egyptians were not pleased with the offer. They carped at it because they were against alliance of any kind, and because the conditions required of them spelt mistrust and inequality instead of what some of them were hoping for —good faith and goodwill. Later, their negotiations with London were to break down over the Sudan, both bilaterally and after their abortive appeal to the United Nations; they overcalled their hand by weaving into their case demands which most nations thought extravagant about limiting the Sudan's right to self-determination. But this topic was merely the immediate cause of failure to reach a settlement with Britain. The real cause was national antipathy to the Suez base. None of the weak coalitions that governed Egypt between the war and the Egyptian revolution could have accepted Britain's minimum military requirements; for Britain could offer nothing that could be presented to the public, to Parliament or even to King Farouk as compensation for a continuing right to re-occupy Egyptian soil.

There is a yardstick by which this assertion can be measured—the fate of Mr Bevin's similar negotiations with Jordan and Iraq. With Jordan he was successful, but then Jordan was differently placed from Egypt and he was in a position to offer compensations. Quite apart from the fact that it was an absolute monarchy and did as King Abdullah said, it was poor, it was small and its money needs were within the range of the British exchequer. Further, its anglophiles could make a good case for guarantees and armaments because of nervousness about Zionist aspirations to its territory. It therefore signed in March 1946 —that is, two months before the British offer to quit Egypt—a treaty not of the new pattern (providing for evacuation with re-activation clauses that would become operative in the event of war) but of the old pre-war type that allowed Britain to station its troops in a foreign country. For this departure from the aspirations of all Arab nationalist parties, King Abdullah came in for sharp Arab criticism behind closed doors at home, but in public abroad. At the meeting of the third session of the Arab League, held in March–April, his Lebanese and Syrian neighbours pointed to the unsuitable contrast between their own rejoicings over British and French evacuation and Jordan's move in the opposite direction. The Arab League pact, they said, precluded agreements without the League's consent. King Abdullah took no notice, but he had committed an offence by nationalist standards, though just how much it went against the grain with some of his own subjects did not become obvious until he had increased the nationalist element among them by taking over Arab Palestine, and half a million Arab refugees, in 1950.

Mr Bevin's negotiations with Iraq followed a different course, but likewise suggest that the Bevin idea of a bargain struck between partners was a pipe-dream. They took place in the winter of 1947–8. In the matter of readiness to listen to British offers, Iraq stood somewhere between Egypt and Jordan. Money compensations were not of the same account to it as to Jordan, for Iraq had become a creditor country as a result of the war, and in June 1945 held a sterling balance in London of about £70 million. (The corresponding British liability to Egypt was £396 million.) It also knew that it could expect a big revenue from oil. But this lay some years ahead, and meanwhile Iraq was (as Egypt also was, and Jordan is not) a country owning potential resources, and impatient to spend its gains on equipment, having been starved of capital goods throughout the war. Yet—and here was another handicap for Mr Bevin—Britain, being likewise starved, could offer Arab creditors neither quick deliveries of goods nor unlimited convertibility of their sterling in order to buy elsewhere. Egypt left the sterling area in dudgeon in 1947, and was offered only moderate financial sweeteners to treaty negotiations until 1951;[3] to Iraq, with its friendlier face and lesser needs, the British forthwith showed "almost quixotic generosity";[4] at the height of Britain's own convertibility crisis, which coincided with the preliminaries to a new treaty, Iraq was handed £15 million in currency immediately convertible.

In any case, the oligarchy that ruled Iraq had better reason than Egypt's to feel anxious about Soviet expansion. It was friendly with Turkey, where many of its leading men had been educated, and it had experienced at only one remove the Soviet pressures of 1945–6

[3] *Financial Times*, July 2, 1947.   [4] *The Times*, August 21, 1947.

on eastern Anatolia and Persian Azerbaijan; both these places were within easy flying distance of its own rich oilfield at Kirkuk. Britain was offering armaments and military and air force training; disregarding the wishes of a small urban middle class that regarded these merely as props for the class in power, an Iraqi team went to Britain in January 1948 to sign a modern replacement for their old, unequal treaty.

It is possible that the Iraqis could have been further tempted (as the Egyptians of the day would not have been) by some British undertaking to support the Arab case over Palestine. Later in 1948, Nuri Pasha was to refer to some such "special arrangement" in a pamphlet called *Facts concerning recent affairs in Iraq and Palestine* which he published, in Arabic, in the summer. But no British official recollects any such offer, nor was one likely from a government that was going to extraordinary lengths to be neutral over Palestine at the United Nations. How could such a proposition be made by a country dependent, for survival, on an American loan and on American co-operation in the struggle with the Soviet Union over Germany, at this time approaching its height? It is probable that some chance remark, or even a silence, while Nuri, armed with a map in Claridges, expounded to an eminent British audience Arab military plans for cutting Jewish Palestine in two, was later magnified into an "offer" in order to whitewash some of the mixed bag of Iraqi politicians who had been to Britain.

In contrast to all the British attempts to come to an agreement with pre-revolutionary Egypt, the Portsmouth Treaty with Iraq very nearly succeeded. It was signed, after a lunch held on board Nelson's *Victory*, by several important Iraqi statesmen. Yet, through their over confidence and London's, the publicity for it was bungled, and, by stages that lasted over some days, their enemies in Baghdad raised a mob and frightened the Regent into announcing that it did not realize the country's aspirations (which was true if the "country" was the nationalists). So it was thrown out.

Admittedly, there were several reasons for this rebuff, among them a famine, and the coincidence of the signature with a moment of Arab wrath and fear about Palestine; the British reasons for this timing will be described later. But in Iraq, as in every other Arabic-speaking state that aspired to call itself a democracy, the main impulse at work in everyone under fifty was resistance to British efforts to modernize the basis of military occupation or re-occupation. Mr Bevin was trying to swim against the strongest current of opinion in the area, was buffeted by it, and was obliged to fall back on the unexpired residue of pre-war agreements. The local accompaniments to his policy were hostile press and radio comment wherever there was no censor, and occasional demonstrations by Arab crowds, though it remained easy for Englishmen to keep up amicable intercourse with Arab nationalists in private life. In 1948, both the former slights were bearable by a power that was girding itself for a near-war situation over Berlin.

For in the interval between the abortive offer to quit Egypt in May 1946 and that to quit Iraq in January 1948, the political situation in Europe had greatly changed for the worse. It had never been good from the moment in 1944 when the Russians had first revealed, in Rumania, that they meant nothing that the west meant by the Yalta Declaration on Liberated Europe. In 1946, the political decision to offer evacuation to Egypt would never have been made had not other Middle Eastern bases been available.

The word "bases" includes not only the apparatus of GHQ, but storage and repair facilities. When the offer to evacuate Egypt was made, two other sites were envisaged. These were Palestine as a whole, with its excellent port, oil pipe-line and refinery at Haifa and, as a dump for heavy equipment that might be handier if stored in Africa than in Britain, a railway halt in Kenya called McKinnon Road. Where GHQ was to go was still unsettled when the Egyptian treaty fell through. The Royal Air Force would have been content with Cyprus; the army naturally favoured the mainland. But in 1946 Palestine was to be the main substitute for Suez, and the soldiers started on the enormous job of shifting square miles of war stores from Egypt both to there and to Kenya.

The move began in spite of the fact that Palestine was already a scene of rebellion owing to British refusal to allow unlimited Jewish immigration; it was on July 22, 1946, that the Irgun Zvai Leumi blew up British military headquarters in the King David Hotel. But British army commanders are inured to unpopularity; they are ready to face an inordinate amount of local opposition and creation of inconvenience before they admit that a base is too hot to hold. The movement of troops and goods entailed by this Palestine-cum-Kenya scheme continued until the date in September 1947 when the British Colonial Secretary announced that Britain was abandoning the Palestine Mandate.

By that time, new conditions at home and in Europe had begun to affect British cabinet judgements of what was feasible. By late 1946, world commodity prices were rising to a height that gravely reduced the purchasing power of the American loan negotiated on exacting terms in 1945, and Mr Bevin's financial colleagues—Dr Dalton at the Exchequer and Sir Stafford Cripps at the Board of Trade—were demanding changes of plan. Notably, they were asking for less feeding of Germany and less expenditure on troops in political outposts abroad:

"Week by week and day by day he (Hugh Dalton) had to come to the cabinet to report on the dollar position. It was not his fault. It was not anybody's fault. It was the fault of events, and it became perfectly clear with the rise in prices that sooner or later an enormous change in our whole position would have to be faced."[5]

In the Middle East, the first of several enormous changes was Mr Bevin's capitulation to Treasury pressure for military economies in Greece and Turkey. After a pause that was due to his sense of timing—he wanted to be sure that the Americans would stop the gap—the facts were stated in Washington; the United States was asked to take over the burden of financial-military support for the resistance of these two countries to Soviet pressure. Secretary of the Navy Forrestal records that the cabinet received the demand with consternation:

". . . Marshall said that this dumped in our lap another most serious problem—that it was tantamount to British abdication from the Middle East with obvious implications as to their successor."[6]

But the timing was good, and the Americans responded with the celebrated Truman Doctrine of March 12, 1947. The date was a red-letter day, and is denied this rank only by the school of British imperialists who leave out of account Britain's loss of money and resources, and therefore of power, as a result of the war. It is a turning point in British Middle Eastern history, for after it, as General Marshall at once foresaw, responsibility for Middle Eastern defence against Russia was a shared, as opposed to a single-handed, task.

Simultaneously, a second enormous change was taking place on the eastern side of the area. By rights, the independence of India should have reduced Britain's sense of responsibility for policing the classic passage through the Middle East. But habits die hard, and the British passage to India is also the Soviet gateway to Africa. In 1947, relations with the Soviet Union were growing so bad in Europe that the

[5] Mr Bevin to the Labour Party Conference, Scarborough, May 20, 1948.

[6] *The Forrestal Diaries.* Edited by Walter Millis (London, 1952), p. 242 (entry for February 24, 1947).

S.A.P.—B

British Imperial General Staff thought of the change as an amputation:

> "With the loss of India and Burma the keystone of the arch of our Commonwealth Defence was lost", wrote Lord Alanbrooke in his *Notes on my Life*. "Without the central strategic reserve of Indian troops able to operate either east or west, we were left impotent. . . ."[7]

No money; no Palestine; no India; and a very grave possibility of war with the Soviet Union over Berlin. It was on March 5, 1948 (that is, just two months before the Palestine war), that the American military governor in Germany sent home his prescient and alarming telegram about "a subtle change in the Soviet attitude which I cannot define but which now gives me a feeling that it (war) may come with dramatic suddenness. I cannot support this change in my own thinking with any data or outward evidence in relationships other than to describe it as a new tenseness in every Soviet individual with whom we have official relations."[8]

A week later, Mr Bevin was communicating to Washington his deep apprehension "over the evident intention of the Soviet Union to bring immediate pressure upon Norway to negotiate a pact similar to that which they are now asking of Finland", and was wanting to discuss an extension of the five-nation Brussels Pact, a plan for Atlantic security and a Mediterranean system of security. The Americans were not yet ready for these large ideas[9] and the winter of 1947–8 was the lowest point in the dip of Britain's post-war fortunes. A black outlook was mitigated only by American appearance in strength in the Mediterranean, and the hope offered by the Marshall plan with its dollar aid for Europeans who were ready to help themselves. But if that plan was to restore European industry and check the westward spread of want, idleness and communism, oil that could be paid for in soft currencies was a necessity. An important ingredient of it was a steady flow of Middle Eastern oil.

We know now that the best way to make sure of this is to pay the Arab or Persian ground landlord a price he cannot afford to drop, but in 1947 this conception had not dawned in the west; nor had any of the Arab states or Persia embarked on the social programmes that nowadays make them unable to forfeit recurring income. Military strength

[7] Arthur Bryant, *Triumph in the West. Completing the War Diaries of Field Marshal Viscount Alanbrooke* (London, 1959), p. 533.

[8] *The Forrestal Diaries*, p. 367.   [9] *Ibid.*, pp. 371–2.

on the spot was thought to be more effective. Even the Americans, operating on sensibly short leases that looked less permanent, and therefore more inviting, to Arab nationalists than Britain's old-fashioned "twenty-years-renewable" propositions, had retained an air base that dated from the war on the perimeter of the Arabian American Oil Company's field at Dhahran in Saudi Arabia. The British, with their much longer tradition of a chain of Middle Eastern strongpoints, hung on to everything to which they had rights. Deprived of Palestine by the surrender of the mandate in May 1948, they fell back on the unexpired Egyptian treaty and the Canal Zone. An idea that they would be wise to concentrate their forces farther south in Africa[10] lost ground when General Smuts failed to win the South African election of May 1948.

The British planners on the Canal knew that, in the event of war over Germany, troops and equipment would be short in western Europe, and the Middle East was likely to be a secondary theatre. If these forecasts were correct, they could expect no reinforcements. They therefore made what dispositions they could under their own steam. Of the local governments, Transjordan was the only sure ally; during 1947-8 they greatly improved the armament of the Arab Legion (which was, in their view, till then only of desert police standard) and strengthened its complement of British officers. They acted without time or thought for the Zionist view of this move.

The British military planners were also anxious to do work on Iraqi airfields and get flying experience there. It was largely under pressure from them that the Foreign Office pushed ahead with arrangements for a new Iraqi treaty in the autumn of 1947, regardless of a scene in Palestine that was the opposite of propitious. For the plan of the time was—in the event of war—to sabotage Abadan refinery and, if need be, also the oilfields of the Persian Gulf region, and for as long as possible to use Iraqi airfields to fly strikes into south Russia, and to delay Russian ground troops in the Persian mountains. In the longer run there was to be no attempt to hold more than the line from the Taurus mountains to Aqaba. The American Mediterranean fleet shared in the planning to these ends, from the standpoint of which the bitter Anglo-American quarrel over the birth of Israel in May 1948 could not have been more inopportune. The quick recovery by both nations of a sense of proportion was chiefly due to Stalin and his decision to beseige Berlin, where the Soviet blockade began in June.

[10] Cf. "Africa or the Middle East", Chapter XXIV in B. H. Liddell Hart, *Defence of the West* (London, 1950).

Although Mr Bevin had nothing to offer that Arabs wanted, except arms in quantities that the larger Arab states thought paltry, and although he was denying them their real desire, which was complete freedom to plan their own defence and foreign policy, they did not turn their backs on Britain. Its relationship to them was beginning to alter, in that it was a debtor instead of a creditor, and was no longer their only foreign recourse in matters of bounty and political support. Yet changes of this kind were difficult to perceive during the years of shaking-down after the war, and both the Egyptians and the Iraqis kept on doing deals with London; they grumbled, but were conservative, and their conservatism helped to promote at the British end the illusion that the alliances Britain wanted could be helped on by giving economic and technical aid:

"You need us for your defence; you need us for our technical ability; you need us for many things", said Mr Bevin to the Egyptians in 1945. "We need you too equally. . . . I hope Anglo-Egyptian relationships will never, from today, carry an idea that we are the predominant partner."[11]

But the whole conception of aid was stunted by the fact that Britain wanted bases. By Egyptian and Arab standards, foreign aid was necessary and desirable, but the only helpers whom nationalists felt able to welcome without reserve were those to whom they paid an ordinary market wage for their services; consultant engineering firms, notably, were hired without suspicion on grounds of nationality. Aid from governments was in another class, and if coming from government with pretensions to political power in the area, was in a class apart. Britain was especially suspect, and seldom got credit even where some credit for selflessness was due.

Mr Bevin certainly did not do so. Yet he is worth an Arab thought in that his aid schemes were far the earliest to be offered, and were prompted not just by British self-interest, but by his heartfelt feeling that "we have added very great wealth to the country (Egypt), but it has never flowed down to the fellahin".[12]

Mr Bevin's conception of diplomacy was to produce what he called a "real harmony between the growing aspirations of the whole of the masses of the people of the world and a higher standard of life".[13] His

[11] At a lunch commemorating Alamein, October 23, 1945.
[12] House of Commons, May 24, 1946.
[13] To an International Conference of Agricultural Producers, May 20, 1946.

tragedy was that he had neither the money nor the men for the job. Over three years before President Truman's justly famous "Point IV" speech turned foreign aid into a stock phrase in all languages, he set up a British Middle East Office with a representative in London to recruit technicians, and a small pool of technical experts in Cairo for loan to governments. These were men of wide local experience and the organization was excellent in shape; its technicians, once borrowed, were men familiar with the local problems and the language, and so wasted no time (as the outsider coming in on short term is apt to do) on learning how to work with Arab officials who resent him until he has spent months winning their confidence. The B.M.E.O. had the advantage that its staff were familiars; all over the world, this is a big asset in uneducated communities. Its handicap was its small size; a staff of only six or eight men was a drop in the bucket; further, in the years just after the war, though the Arabs themselves were ready to hire foreigners, good technicians were at a premium in England and unready to take up the short-term appointments that were all local governments wanted to offer.

In any case, all such efforts meet with nationalist resistance. Although the socialist and economic inspiration behind the B.M.E.O. was meant to be patent (its first chief came from the Board of Trade), it most unsuitably shared quarters with diplomats handling overall Arab political questions, such as Palestine. (During 1947, visitors were felt for weapons—the weapons with which Jewish terrorists hoped to shoot their *bête noire*, Brigadier Clayton.) The office, while it remained in Egypt, was housed in a building to which clung an aroma of war-time bossiness and dominance, and Egyptian nationalist feeling against taking its advice was so strong that its services were never officially called in; in most other countries of the area there are little monuments to its work.

But benefits of this kind are not of a nature to pave the way for defence agreements in countries longing to be quit of foreigners, and—as the Egyptians and Arabs of Mr Bevin's day were—mindful of the economic dictation which they had suffered at the hands of the British during the war; the war-time Middle East Supply Centre had had to force them to change many of their habits in order to save shipping. Further, except for a small upper class, war-time inflation had sent living standards down, not up; Egypt in 1947 was eating fewer calories per head than before the war. It is patent that the kind of social developments to which Mr Bevin would have liked Britain to contribute were outside the range of his achievement.

If he approached the Arabs empty-handed (or worse than empty-handed, for he was obliged by Britain's position in Europe to importune them for privileges that only a few old warriors such as King Abdullah and Nuri Pasha were ready to concede), how did he get the name for pursuing an "Arab policy"? He won it over the Palestine problem. Did he deserve it? The question is worth asking in the light of the many outside happenings that swayed Palestine policy.

The topic of Palestine absorbs an amount of print that is out of proportion to its share as an element in British policy. In the years of Mr Bevin's foreign secretaryship it preoccupied and baffled the cabinet, and even on one or two occasions threw a body normally harmonious into argument. But at no point did Palestine constitute a matter of life and death for the United Kingdom balance of payments or standard of living, or for British military security or Commonwealth relations as did, in 1947, the convertibility crisis or the India Act or, in 1948, the siege of Berlin. Its effect on Anglo-American relations at a time when Britain could not survive without American financial and strategic support was its only vital impact on practical policy. Its moral implications were another matter. Its effect on Anglo-Jewish and Anglo-Arab relations were deeply embittering. But in the Arabic-speaking world it was not at that time the prime cause of bitterness except in Syria (which bore Britain no grudges about occupation or tutelage) and, of course, among the Palestinians. Egypt, to the annoyance of the other members of the Arab League, gave first priority to securing total, permanent British evacuation, and even Iraq threw out the Portsmouth Treaty less because of Palestine (about which the Kurdish fifth of the population did not care) than on account of personal rivalries bound up with dislike of pro-British moves.

Profitless though it is to speculate about the might-have-been, it is doubtful if, even had Mr Bevin been able to stick to the 1939 White Paper limiting Jewish immigration, his recompense would have been the military privileges and Arab goodwill that were his goal. However, those who think he should have done so are apt to forget that pressure to mitigate the plight of the Jews did not come only from America; it was an element in British policy also. The Labour Party had long-standing sympathies with Zionism; jettisoning the Jews to win Arab favours was out of the question, and anything short of this was bound by Arab standards to be less than ideal. A respite from Arab antagonism—even a temporary spell of popularity—might have been gained, but any British policy that took the Jewish problem into sympathetic account was bound in the not so long run to lead back into the old mire.

Mr Bevin's name for pro-Arab leanings was therefore earned for a policy that was never pro-Arab in Arab eyes. His name for bias came from non-Arabs—from all Jews, most Americans and many Englishmen. Yet, at least until 1948, his policy if examined in the context of all Britain's problems of the day, is not a pro-Arab but a pro-British policy. It is firmly rooted in home opinion, in Britain's financial and strategic lot, and in the physical and political wellbeing of British and European workers who seldom if ever gave Palestine a thought.

In one respect Palestine, seen from between the blinkers which most of us were apt to wear when we looked at it, was different from all the other problems that crossed Mr Bevin's desk. It presented few or no complications over relations with the Soviet Union. The Soviet government of his day was bent merely on making Middle Eastern snags more awkward for the west, without heed as to whether each act favoured Arab or Jew. (Hence what was, in Arab and Jewish eyes, an unpredictable distribution of Soviet votes and supporting gestures.) Marshal Stalin had told Mr Bevin, during a private and informal talk in the Kremlin on March 24, 1947, held in the course of the Moscow Conference of Foreign Ministers, that he did not intend to interfere with British policy in the Middle East.[14] The talk took place less than a fortnight after the Truman doctrine had been announced, and it is clear that a condition of the undertaking was, in Stalin's mind, "provided the Americans are kept out of it". At the time, separation of British from United States policy was a major Soviet objective.

When Mr Bevin took up the threads of the Palestine problem in its congenitally impossible shape, the Coalition Government had discussed it and come to no decision about it, though it had favoured partition.[15] A Labour cabinet sub-committee, of which he was chairman, was appointed in August 1945 to consider what to do about the 1939 White Paper. This the Party had consistently opposed, but the sub-committee seems to have decided that it could not be rescinded until there was an alternative policy to put in its place. Yet the problem of the Jews in DP camps pressed; the sub-committee therefore advocated carrying on with a small monthly issue of Jewish immigration visas even after the remaining balance of the White Paper quota was exhausted. Meanwhile the British cabinet battled with American pressure to do much more than this, while urging Washington to agree

[14] Lord Strang, *At Home and Abroad* (London, 1956), p. 260; and Jon Kimche, *Seven Fallen Pillars* (London, 1953), p. 72.

[15] Mr Oliver Stanley, House of Commons, July 31, 1946; and Lord Alanbrooke's diary for November 6, 1944, quoted in Arthur Bryant, *op. cit.*, p. 321.

that the problem of displaced Jews was far too large to be met by Palestine alone. The sub-committee did not pursue the alternative of partition, chiefly on the grounds that this could only be carried out by force, which was the opinion of most of the ambassadors in the Arab capitals, with their natural concern for the wider aspects of British Middle Eastern alliances. By and large, the partition solution was for this reason throughout disliked by the Foreign Office, whereas the Colonial Office saw it as the least of a series of evils because it would preserve at least something of the constructive work of a generation.

But the use of force, which had always been repugnant, was in 1945 out of the question, chiefly because the British public had had enough of soldiering, but also because force would have struck a false note if used by those who were contesting the Soviet Union's right to enforce solutions on Eastern Europe. And Mr Bevin's personal instincts were all against it because of the faith he placed in negotiating with foreigners. About this he knew a lot; he had had years of touch-and-go experience with wayward trade unions not only in Britain but all over Europe, and he had supreme confidence in his own capacity as a negotiator. He often referred to the settlements that could be reached at the eleventh hour and the fifty-ninth minute, and these experiences account for his well remembered "personal assurance" to Mr Barnet Janner in the House of Commons that he would "stake my political future" on solving the problem of Palestine.[16] The remark was not made on impulse; he made it also to the Jewish leaders, and to a meeting which he summoned of the Fleet Street diplomatic correspondents.

But in making it he underrated how desperate, and therefore how uncompromising, are communities which see reason to fear extinction. He set out to get a compromise because he thought he could do it, because compromise over a unitary Palestine suited the British Imperial General Staff at a time of pressure on the Middle East by Soviet Russia, and because of his own dreams of world betterment. "I firmly believe that apart altogether from a solution of the Palestine problem and not as a substitute for it, there would be a great welcome for many Jewish brains and ability throughout the whole of the Arab world."[17] To get his ends, he induced the 1945 cabinet to add the Americans to the fray. The suggestion was all his own, and was made without consulting his officials (whom it threw into consternation because it offered the Americans a say without corresponding responsibility). But he over-

[16] House of Commons, November 13, 1945.
[17] To the Labour Party Conference, Bournemouth, June 12, 1946.

rode them because he thought that the Americans were more likely than the British to influence the Zionists to be reasonable. He anticipated common ground with the United States because it too was concerned to counter Soviet expansion, and he thought that two powers would be better than one at finding accommodation for the Jewish displaced persons, for all of whom anyone dispassionate was bound to reckon that there was not room in Palestine.

At the time, there were good grounds for thinking this reasoning valid. Both the Pentagon, and later the State Department, had during the war shown they were alive to the strategic and political liabilities of controversy in Palestine, and had stopped discussion by Congress of pro-Zionist resolutions.[18] The liabilities had not ended with the war, because of western uncertainty about Russia's Middle East intentions at a time of pressure on both Turkey and Persia. Further, two American Presidents who had handled the subject of Palestine—Truman as well as Roosevelt—had, while sympathetic to Zionism, given their word to Arab enquirers not to act without consulting the Arabs. There was much evidence to suggest that British and American concern to hold a balance between Jew and Arab would be identical.

Factors that the British cabinet left out of account, or underrated, when they invited American advice without American liability for executing it were first, American anti-imperialism, with its accompanying suspicions of British motives in wanting to hold on to overseas territories; second, the influence of American history on American sympathy with pioneers opening up a new home for the free;[19] third, the capacity of the American Zionists to turn all effort to succour European Jewry into effort to found a Jewish state in Palestine; and fourth, the strong case to be presented by the European desks of the State Department for getting the DP camps cleared at the earliest possible moment. A crowning factor that no one could foresee was how much more readily this President would listen to Zionist friends and advisers than to the State Department officials who were urging him to remember the Arabs.

But there was contemporary evidence of the first two elements. American mistrust of British motives overseas had been loudly expressed when British troops were landed in Greece in 1944; and, at the end of the war, the Anglo-American joint arrangements for a Middle East Supply centre did not survive largely because of American suspicions of British motives in an underdeveloped area that was also in

[18] Cordell Hull, *Memoirs* (London, 1948), Vol. II, p. 1534.
[19] Cf. R. H. S. Crossman, *Palestine Mission* (London, 1946), p. 42.

the sterling area. The American citizen of 1945 thought British power politics more dastardly than Russian ones.

As to Zionism, no one in London had measured the extent to which (as a combined result of the 1939 White Paper and of the war) the Zionists had shifted their propaganda effort from Britain to the United States. By 1945, they were no longer causing pressure on the British government by rousing American opinion; they were directly pressing the United States to take action, and were doing it through bodies that had become much more powerful than the old Emergency Committees in London and Jerusalem. Their capacity for turning all Jewish rescue work to Zionist account had been evident during a move by President Roosevelt in 1943 to get his Jewish friend Morris Ernst to run a campaign for settling Jewish refugees in welcoming countries everywhere; American Zionists had turned on Ernst "as if I were a traitor" and he had had to drop the work.[20]

Possibly the British cabinet underrated these factors because, in the mind of most people at the time, the image of the Jew was that of a victim rather than of a driving-force; undoubtedly the familiar figure of Dr Weizmann, still circling round his eminent British friends, led them to suppose that the nature of Zionist pressure had not changed; most of all, they were ill-informed because there was at the time no office or person responsible for measuring and reporting on Jewish activities outside Palestine. It was not the job of the Colonial Office, and when the embassy in Washington sent comment to the American Division of the Foreign Office, there seems to have been an inclination to write off as pro-Zionist those (among them the ambassador, Lord Inverchapel) who stressed Zionist strength in the United States.

On balance American participation in the Commission of Enquiry of 1945/6 was an asset. Mr Bevin so firmly thought so that he undertook, to the twelve members when they were on their way through London to the Middle East in December 1945, to implement any report that was unanimous. Though he did this on impulse after a lunch, and had no power to bind the cabinet, they took him at his word.

The Israelis, for whom Mr Bevin became a Titus or a Haman, are convinced that he was against them from the start, and there is evidence in 1946 that he was sensitive to the rumour that he was anti-Jewish, for he went out of his way at the Labour Party conference of that year to recall his record at the Whitechapel election of 1931, which should have dispelled it. There is no evidence that he embarked on the Palestine problem with a prejudice against the Jews; his undertaking to

[20] Morris Ernst, *So Far So Good* (New York, 1948), pp. 170–7.

execute a unanimous report is that of a fair-minded man, and all his published words suggest that he was just as concerned as President Truman to get the DP camps emptied of Jews as quickly as of their other inmates. But he was quick-tempered and often short with people who saw problems only from their own angle. What he early began to resent was the attitude that had so deeply exercised Morris Ernst— the Zionist refusal to succour Jewry in any way but the Zionist way of exodus to Palestine.

Hence the two remarks which set going the Zionist theory that he was quarrelsome, inhumane, and responsive only when he wanted something. Both remarks are quoted with this comment by Dr Weizmann in his memoirs. The one was made to a press conference, that "if the Jews, with all their suffering, want to get too much to the head of the queue, you have the danger of another anti-semitic reaction through it all"; the other was made to Weizmann personally about a number of immigration certificates to Palestine which the Jews considered too insignificant to accept: "What do you mean by refusing certificates? Are you trying to force my hand? If you want a fight you can have it!"[21] The brusque tone was one that he often used to people whom he thought unready to see that he had grasped their point. Prejudice developed later, and was cumulative. Before 1945, he had not given the subject much attention. But immediately he started reading the Foreign Office files, he felt vexed with the Zionists in the Labour Party for playing a confidence trick on the rank and file when they pushed through the party conference in 1944 a recommendation so heedless of overall British interests as that which recommended that "the Arabs be encouraged to move out, as the Jews move in". Also in his early days, he felt contempt for the technique of Jewish Agency representatives who officially denied that the Agency had anything to do with violent acts by the Hagana when proof of complicity lay on his desk.[22] But these were small matters; the first factor of importance was his exasperation at the nature of pressure from New York and Washington, and few besides Zionists see proof that bias was there from the beginning.

The motives which governed his policy from the first were unashamedly pro-British. He favoured a unitary state (which the Zionists did not want) because it was the solution most likely to suit the defence arrangements for which the cabinet was striving, and which have

[21] Chaim Weizmann, *Trial and Error* (London, 1949), p. 541.
[22] Cmd. 6873 of 1946 (*Palestine: Statement of Information relating to Causes of Violence*) made part of the evidence public.

already been described. He thought (as President Roosevelt had come to
think after his talks with Arab kings on his way back from Yalta just
before his death)[23] that a Jewish state in Palestine could be established
and maintained only by force, and that force would send the Arabs
hotfoot to Moscow. Also, he thought it a mistake to create two states
neither of which would be viable.

When the report of the Anglo-American Commission of Enquiry
came out on May 1, 1948, it fulfilled Mr Bevin's principal requirements. It was unanimous, it recommended a unitary state, and it had
American moral and financial backing for its execution. Yet the
British cabinet never endorsed the Bevin promise and turned the report
down. Why? One valid explanation is that offered by one of the
several members who wrote books about it, Mr R. H. S. Crossman,
who judges that:

> "Our report could not have been submitted at a more inopportune
> moment. The Peace Conference was just beginning; Mr Bevin was
> in Paris and the Government was harassed by a mountain of crises,
> including the Egyptian and Indian negotiations, as well as the
> Russian deadlock. Palestine was just something extra on an over-
> crowded plate, and it was dealt with hurriedly."[24]

He adds with justice that it was therefore turned over for comment to
the very officials whose evidence to the Commission had pointed in
other directions.

Another motive, always present from 1945 onwards, was unwillingness to use force to impose a solution, not merely out of public distaste
for it, but because of its cost. The men on the spot reported that the
immediate admission of an extra 100,000 Jews would call for an additional British division; for how long, they could not say. The Chancellor of the Exchequer said there were no funds available; in 1946, he
was hard put to it to find the £40 million that the British exchequer
spent on feeding Germany; new and heavy expenditure on Palestine
would have been difficult to explain to a British public that was, owing
to the rising price of food grains, being introduced to bread rationing
for the first time in its history.

Hurry over a decision that calls for measured thought often breeds
annoyance; the annoyance was exacerbated by President Truman's
precipitate adoption of a single provision (the immediate issue of

[23] Cf. a State Department memorandum to the new President, quoted in
H. S. Truman, *Memoirs* (London, 1956), Vol. II, p. 133.
[24] R. H. S. Crossman, *op. cit.*, p. 200.

100,000 Jewish immigration certificates) out of ten interlocking recommendations. Tension over the contemporary offer (May 7) to evacuate Egypt was very great. Yet judgement went astray when the British cabinet allowed itself to grow testy with the Americans for placing burdens on Britain without lifting a finger to help enforce the scheme; in its annoyance, it reasoned as if Britain had a wealth of alternatives to the course proposed. Whether or no the solution offered was the best of a bad bunch is beside the point. It is a golden rule of life than an imperfect decision, boldly undertaken, produces a better result than no decision at all; the axiom was stated by Mr Churchill during a debate on later discussions with the Americans on an alternative plan:

"It is far more important that there should be agreement than that there should be this or that variant of the scheme. Any solution in which the U.S.A. would join us could be made to work."[25]

Had the British cabinet been less busy and irritable, it might have noticed some writing on the wall. The commission had reached unanimity only by a hair's breadth. During its final discussions in Lausanne, three of its members had come out in favour of partition (Macdonald, Crossman and Crum); two others (Singleton and Manningham-Buller) had been of the opinion that issue of an immediate 100,000 Jewish immigration certificates ought to depend on the calling off of Jewish terrorism. All the Americans thought this proviso impracticable. These five men waived their convictions because they placed first things first and went for a solution that would be executed quickly. The two last did so only when reminded afresh of Mr Bevin's undertaking to execute the report if it were unanimous. The reminder, which was given at Mr Crossman's insistence, came from Mr Noel Baker, at the time a Minister of State for Foreign Affairs, who was in Geneva winding up the League of Nations.

Once the Bevin undertaking was not kept, these potential dissidents naturally felt free to express other views. They had worked hard and become experts; their advice was likely to be sought in the future by members of the executive and legislature in both countries. Never again would it be unanimous. The effect of British over-confidence in British powers in May 1946 was to allow the initiative to pass to those who knew their minds. From then on, all other British proposals were doomed.

This fate was not at once apparent. As if Anglo-American relations

[25] House of Commons, August 1, 1946.

were unimpaired by Mr Bevin's impolitic quip to the Labour Party conference in June 1946, that President Truman had been so insistent on the immediate 100,000 certificates because "they didn't want too many Jews in New York", both states appointed cabinet committees to thrash out a new joint plan. But the bloom had gone off joint effort, and the alternative, called the Morrison-Grady plan, merely amounted to an attempt by the Colonial Office to recover the initiative. Though acceptable to the American diplomats who framed it, it was a hopeless proposition to put to the White House. For the President very naturally consulted the members of the earlier commission, who were against it; in addition, his staff and his close personal friends included many ardent pro-Zionists who backed them up; as a member of the State Department was ruefully to tell the British Ambassador when the latter pressed Mr Acheson for the President's support for the plan, not a member of either House of Congress would feel able to back it, or the President on it.

Time was not improving Mr Bevin's chances. More than a year had elapsed since VE Day, and mounting Jewish impatience had led to mounting terrorism in Palestine, followed by the kind of British counter-action from which it is difficult to step down unless the terrorism stops. Nevertheless, that summer of 1946 was a low moment for the Zionists; their way to statehood did not look at all clear. Meeting in Paris, their leaders decided on retreat from the demand framed in the Biltmore resolutions of 1942, which had stipulated that the whole of Palestine be recognized as a Jewish commonwealth, and on readiness to discuss a Jewish state in a viable area of Palestine.

A combination of these events reduced Mr Bevin's hold on the course of events to zero. His four subsequent efforts to initiate a compromise were all useless. The Morrison-Grady plan (which implied indefinitely prolonging British rule) had foundered on the rocks of American anti-imperialism as well as American antipathy to the line the British were taking about immediate Jewish immigration. The London Conference which followed it—attended by no Jews and no Palestinian Arabs because these would not come unless represented by the Mufti—was the beginning of an abortive attempt to convince un-believing Arab states that Palestine would do better at British hands than at those of an international forum. When Mr Bevin held private talks with Jewish leaders from Palestine and New York, which he did in Paris in August and in London two months later "there was a feeling . . . that I had the right approach at last".[26] But the feeling was all

[26] House of Commons, February 25, 1947.

his own, and was misplaced. He put down his failure to a speech that President Truman made on the Jewish Day of Atonement, and which was timed out of eagerness to forestall a Zionist statement by Mr Dewey in connexion with the forthcoming New York election.[27] The President maintains that this speech was consistent with his earlier attitude;[28] but in fact it constituted a switch that gave a great lift of heart to the Zionists, for it supported, for the first time, their new policy for a state in part of Palestine. Admittedly it struck a knell for Mr Bevin; it also resulted in the American Secretary of State (Mr Byrnes), who was with Bevin in Paris when it was made, "washing his hands of the whole Palestine matter, which meant that it was allowed to drift without action and practically without any American policy".[29] But Mr Bevin exaggerated when he said that because of it "the whole thing was spoilt".[30] For by the standards of most of the Jews whom he had seen—Weizmann, Goldman, Wise, Locker, Kaplan and others—the talks (which were helped by the fact that Mr Arthur Creech Jones, who had long had sympathy with Zionism, had taken over the Colonial Office) were only a beginning. They were:

"... in the most preliminary stages. There was as yet neither a cup nor any liquor for a cup. There could in fact be nothing of substance until the will was known of the Zionist Congress which met in Bâle on the 9th December."[31]

The outcome of that Congress confirms the theory that Mr Bevin had overrated his chances. It bowed to the determination of its American members to abandon faith in Britain, voting in such a way that Dr Weizmann resigned his leadership.

Mr Bevin's dealings with the Arabs may have been less edgy than those with the Jews, but were no more satisfactory, for here too he could make no offer that came within even remote range of their desires. In the course of his talks with them, both on Palestine and on the treaties that so many of them did not want to sign, he made one or two good friendships—notably, with the Egyptian ambassador in London, Abdel Fattah Amr, with whom he used often to dine and talk of the whole range of home as well as foreign affairs.

"I uttered every warning I could to the Arab governments...." He often referred, after his failure with them, to the uphill, unrewarding

---

[27] *The Forrestal Diaries*, pp. 299 and 332.
[28] Truman, *Memoirs*, Vol. II, p. 154.   [29] *The Forrestal Diaries*, p. 299.
[30] House of Commons, February 25, 1947.
[31] Harry Sacher, *Israel: The Establishment of a State* (London, 1952), p. 71.

nature of the job of trying to persuade them of where their best interests lay, and to their suspicion of Britain's ulterior motives. Some
ulterior motives there were, but these did not take away from the
worth of British advice that the Arab states might not do as well as
they expected if their case were to go before the United Nations. But
one final effort to establish this point, made at a dinner in London in
January 1947, was in vain. Both the Arabs and the Jews rejected the last
British effort at compromise, dated February 7, 1947—a plan which
was Mr Bevin's own work. The British therefore turned their problem
over to the United Nations.

The year 1947 marks such a sharp change in British cabinet decisions
about suiting British purposes over Palestine that the policy is incom-
prehensible unless it is examined in a wide context. In one respect the
Foreign Secretary's job became easier than it had been. For 1947 was
the year in which Soviet doings in Eastern Europe disillusioned most
western admirers of the Soviet Union. Mr Bevin ceased to have to gloss
over motives for wanting bases and needing American support, and the
critics to his left, some of whom had fired off their vehement *Keep
Left* pamphlet at the Party Conference in May, had by the winter of
1947–8 come to admit that, for the moment, getting American support for containing Soviet expansion was the only course to follow.

The events which started this shift in British thinking, and in American thinking also, were the systematic murder of socialists in Eastern
Europe, the establishment of the Cominform in order to dominate the
satellites and breed bad blood with all opponents, and—most telling
of all—the refusal to allow the eastern European countries to participate in the Marshall Plan. "Never in my life was I more disillusioned
than when the Soviet Union delegates walked out of the conference
room at the Quai d'Orsay", Mr Bevin later told his Trade Union
friends.[32] Neither he, nor most of the people who had been criticizing
him for a "Tory" policy over defence and alliances, could get over this
readiness to "injure the health of people already underfed".[33] Both he
and Mr Byrnes had been under fire for opposing Stalin and Molotov,
but Soviet acts of 1947, capped by the Czech coup in February 1948,
did the job of forming a western block on their behalf. Later—when
the Palestine fever had been reduced to normal in American home
politics—Soviet acts drove them also towards shared policies in the
Middle East.

Also during 1947, British Middle Eastern policy was coloured by

[32] To delegates attending the E.R.P. International Trade Union Conference,
March 9, 1948.   [33] House of Commons, June 30, 1948.

financial straits at home. Inability to go on bearing the cost of military aid to Greece and Turkey had led to the Truman Doctrine in the spring. In July, fulfilling the stringent condition about convertibility which the Americans, in their urge to get back to economic liberalism, had imposed when granting their post-war British loan, sterling became convertible. The rush to convert in order to spend in countries which could make early deliveries caused an unbearable drain on sterling. This was so heavy that American consent to suspending convertibility was obtained, and took effect on August 21.

In view of the sharpness of the Anglo-American quarrel over Palestine, it would be astonishing had no financial pressure been exercised in the course of these transactions. But little came about. There had been traces of it during the agonizing debates in Congress on the grant of the loan in July 1946, when some pressure ensued.[34] Again in May 1948, it was suggested that Marshall Aid to Britain should be reconsidered if it were being used indirectly to arm Arabs to fight against a policy favoured by the United States.[35] But neither suggestion greatly altered anyone's behaviour. For the two powers were being driven closer and closer together as the Americans came to be goaded by Soviet policy into stating that they intended to stay in Europe.[36] From that moment, America and Britain were so closely linked over European matters of greater moment than anything that was happening in the Middle East that their Palestine quarrel, though so bitter to both, was vital to neither. However angry Mr Bevin and President Truman became over each other's remarks on Palestine, each always recognized that the other was sound as a rock on the subject of Russia.

When the British government turned its Palestine problem over to the United Nations, defence policy was in the forefront of its mind, and it did not envisage surrender of the mandate. It was still under the illusion that it retained some initiative, and merely asked how its mandate "can be administered . . . or amended". It wanted to hang on for two reasons—first, the strategic one already mentioned, and secondly because it reckoned that its garrisons were a guarantee of steady oil supplies:

> "The British interests in the Middle East contribute substantially not only to the prosperity of the people there but also to the wage packets of the workers in this country."[37]

[34] Cf. *The Forrestal Diaries*, p. 182.
[35] Cf. Congressional Record (Senate), May 21, 1948.
[36] Mr Byrnes announced this at Stuttgart, September 6, 1946.
[37] Mr Bevin, House of Commons, May 16, 1947.

Less than a month after Mr Bevin made this allusion to the relationship of oil supplies payable in sterling to British living standards, General Marshall made, at Harvard on June 5, the speech that Mr Bevin later described as "manna from heaven"[38] and that became the starting point of the Marshall Plan. From July 1947, Middle Eastern oil supplies were worth protecting on behalf of the workers not only of Britain, but of all western Europe.

The sum of all these new factors ought to have added up to the conclusion that a base in Palestine was as important to the west as it had ever been, yet on September 26, 1947, the British announced at the United Nations that they were giving up the Palestine mandate. The decision was a sudden one; military headquarters in the Canal Zone learnt almost overnight that their steady removal of troops and goods from the Canal Zone to Palestine must go into reverse. It seemed so out of keeping with British tradition that few people believed it would be put into effect.

This further "enormous change in our whole position" was not a direct consequence of the verdict of the United Nations Commission on Palestine (UNSCOP) which had issued a majority report favouring partition. The British government's main motives were political and human, and cumulatively they make an impressive list.

One was the force of public opinion at home. The British public had taken Palestine in its stride for years, and had looked on "disturbances" and "violence" there much as it had viewed "the trouble" in Ireland— as an unpleasant experience that was part of the white man's burden. But on August 1, 1947, its attitude changed, and the cause of the change was the hanging of two young sergeants whom Jewish terrorists executed as a reprisal. All home comment on that deed is different in tone from that on earlier terrorist acts, many of which caused greater loss of life—for instance, the blowing up of the officers' club or of the King David Hotel. Picture papers frontpaged photographs of the hanged men; disgust was expressed at the placing of booby traps on their bodies; liberal opinion was exercised over small outbursts of anti-semitism in several British towns. At a most unsuitable moment, the event quickened anti-American feeling, for the excesses which the Zionists had perpetrated in advertising campaigns for funds in America had included remarks which stirred even the stolid British to anger; the one most quoted was that about a song in the heart every time a British soldier was killed. On August 1, the *Daily Mail* appealed to the feelings of "American women whose dollars helped to buy the rope".

[38] To the Foreign Press Association, January 25, 1949.

The cost of Palestine to the home taxpayer also played its part. Between January 1945 and November 30, 1947, the bill was £100 million[39]—a poor return for money at a moment when the British were finding it financially necessary to make further troop withdrawals from southern Europe.[40]

Another thought that weighed with the cabinet in general, and Mr Attlee in particular, was the example of India. There, two hostile communities had been confronted with the urgency of a time limit and left to sort things out for themselves; though they had not at once settled down, the experiment had on the whole been successful. The Indian Independence bill had become law in July.

Another date worth mentioning is August 28, when Egypt had failed to get the Security Council to declare the Anglo-Egyptian treaty of 1936 invalid. This treaty was therefore due to run until 1956, and a British base of a certain size—though of a much smaller size than that to which it had grown—was still, in law, available on the Suez Canal.

There is a human reason to add to these dated entries. The Palestine problem, with its roots in irreconcilable promises and its regular crop of emotional complications, had often landed the British in false positions. For instance, the Labour Party was against the White Paper of 1939 for its unfairness to the Jews, and remained so; from the time it took office, it improved on the immigration provisions of that paper; yet by Jewish standards the Labour government favoured the Arabs. Equally, Mr Bevin was a humane man; he showed more compassion for the lot of the individual foreigner than any other British Foreign Secretary. Yet, over Jewish immigration into Palestine, Mr Truman was able to play him into the position of a British monster confronted by an American saviour.

Misinterpretation of character leads to exasperation, and, sometimes, on from there to acts that are out of character, which further exacerbate the temper. This process can be examined in miniature in the affair of the S.S. *Exodus* in the summer of 1948. The *Exodus* was an unseaworthy hulk to which both the Italian and the French authorities had refused a certificate to proceed to sea with passengers. Nevertheless, Zionist agents contrived to load her with about 4,500 passengers, carrying passports with visas for Colombia, filling her in the French port of Sète at the height of a French transport strike. Though London forewarned the French authorities, the *Exodus* was able to put to

[39] Sir Stafford Cripps, House of Commons, January 20, 1948.
[40] *The Forrestal Diaries*, p. 292 (entry for August 4, 1947).

sea. Even the *Manchester Guardian*—always sympathetic to Zionism—remarked at this stage that:

> "No government responsible for law and order could allow Jewish refugees to enter the country as they please, no matter how sympathetic it might feel. There is more than a touch of racketeering in this business."[41]

The *Exodus* was turned back from Palestine, and its passengers, instead of being parked in camps in Cyprus, as their predecessors had been, were sailed back to France. The French cabinet refused to disembark them forcibly. A Zionist launch circled the ship adjuring them to remain on board, which all but about 100 did. For a week none of the waiting pressmen were allowed on board; when at last they were admitted, it was too late to dispel the Zionist fairy tale that the ship was a "floating Auschwitz". In fact, the only matter of life and death involved was the risk of a storm at sea, which was just as great when the Zionists despatched the *Exodus* as at any other time.

The *Exodus* affair was not an isolated piece of racketeering, and the British government decided to try to rid itself of the embarrassments of illegal immigration by making an example of the ship, which it sent back to Germany. The Zionists had made pawns of the passengers; the British government, immensely provoked, committed the same wrong, and its act of sending Jews back to a former charnel house horrified millions, as no other destination would have done. But the cabinet saw complications in the alternatives—landing the passengers in the United Kingdom or, with poetic justice, sending them to Colombia—and after much heartburning, took the line of least resistance. Zionist propaganda was much better than British propaganda at exploiting its decision, and Mr Bevin was branded with names foreign to his nature.

This story is told at length because it crowns a long series of Zionist —chiefly American Zionist—assaults on his integrity at a time when his effort was honest; one which rankled much with him happened at a football game in New York in December 1946, to which he went just after receiving the freedom of that city. When an announcer, entertaining the crowd at half time, told them that he was there, they booed him; he was much upset, but sat out the match. He was provoked not only by what he felt to be Zionist misjudgement of his efforts but by the influence of American election politics on American pronouncements. "Most of the policy has in recent years been run

[41] July 23, 1948.

from New York, and how can I deal with American nationals: I really cannot."[42]

The Arabs might be maddeningly unrealistic; they were obstinate; they were quarrelling among themselves and one of their chief captains was a proclaimed enemy of Great Britain—the Mufti of Jerusalem. But they never drove him to commit acts which troubled his conscience, and so he came to prefer dealing with them to dealing with Zionists. What is more, his own upbringing and experiences prompted sympathy with a class or community that found it difficult to get a hearing: "I think it is sometimes forgotten that the Arabs are in the world."[43] It was by these routes that he developed the streak of bias and prejudice which Mr Churchill had grounds for castigating by January 1949.[44] But bias strong enough to influence policy dates only from 1947; even then, it does not colour one major motive for the British decision to abandon the Palestine mandate, which was the human one, endorsed by all his colleagues, that it was time others tried their hand and got blamed for doing their best.

From the time of the decision to go British policy alters in quality. It becomes defective both morally and in logic. Perhaps the moral flaw was unavoidable, for as had so often happened in Palestine, conflicting undertakings had been given—the one, to be a loyal and working member of the United Nations, and the other to respect the wishes of the inhabitants of Palestine. Mr Bevin was a person of great attachment to his word, but in the case of his word to the Arabs these two undertakings conflicted; for when the United Nations vote became, by the narrowest of margins, a vote in favour of partition, the Jews were pleased and the Arabs were not. By the standards of many people, the right course for Britain had never been in doubt: "From now on the government's first concern should be to help the United Nations."[45] But in Parliament and the cabinet the rush to do this did not set in until the Palestine war had begun.

During the winter of 1947-8, the course of British cabinet policy is difficult to explain except in terms of a progressive loss of control of the situation in Palestine itself. Its logic was at fault in that it tried to preserve neutrality as between Jew and Arab in a situation in which no

[42] To the Labour Party Conference, Margate, May 29, 1947.

[43] House of Commons, January 26, 1949; cf. R. H. S. Crossman, *op. cit.*, p. 42: "As an Englishman, I was surprised and irritated during the Washington hearings by the almost complete disregard of the Arab case."

[44] House of Commons, January 26, 1949.

[45] *Manchester Guardian* leader: "Time to Go", August 1, 1947.

neutrality was possible. It had said that it was willing to help to execute a solution only if this was agreeable to both parties, and partition was not so. Yet to be passive about the execution of partition was to impede it, and *ipso facto* to take the side of the party that did not want it. Shortly after the U.N. vote was cast, the British government spoke up for transfer of its powers "in an orderly manner", though it admitted that it could do nothing towards this end in the districts that its forces were evacuating.[46] Indeed, in its determination to avoid involvement, it on occasion impeded orderly transfer. For instance, it told the U.N. Palestine commission that it could not facilitate a de-limitation of frontiers on the ground, or the establishment of local militias or authorities, and that it could not allow United Nations commissioners to enter Palestine until a fortnight before its own departure on May 15. It did not ask for a central neutral authority to which to hand over powers until May 3, 1948. It insisted on sole responsibility for law and order, without admitting the consequences of preserving this only in a few wired suburbs and along one or two exit routes for its own forces.

A partial explanation, perhaps, of the anomalies just described is that there were clashes between the vested interests of government departments; such clashes are an ingredient of the policy of all nations more often than their nationals at the time care to admit. In the winter of 1947–8, three British departments were divesting themselves of responsibility on Palestine—the Colonial Office, the War Office, the Foreign Office. The first wanted to salve some of its handiwork from wreckage; the second wanted to extricate its men and material intact; the third, to keep up the British position in the rest of the Arab world. None of the three wanted to be responsible for the life and limb of United Nations representatives. All their conflicting desiderata could not be referred to the cabinet to be reconciled; and so in their confusion at loss of the control they were accustomed to exercise, they took individual decisions and made individual statements that did not dovetail with other British acts, and that did not add up to a policy.[47]

As the British withdrew, therefore, they left the country to warring tribes. Their control diminished sector by sector, and was negligible for at least two months before the handover. By then, private Arab armies were shelling the hills around Jerusalem with Syrian howitzers; Jewish settlements and Arab villages were raiding one another with impunity; Glubb Pasha's Arab Legion was building a secret road from the Jordan valley to the top of the escarpment in Judea, and there was

[46] Mr Creech Jones, House of Commons, December 11, 1947.
[47] Cf. Jon Kimche, *Both Sides of the Hill* (London, 1960), pp. 36–8 and 111–12.

considerable loss of morale among the British troops that remained. Why intervene between armed adversaries if they were going home next week?

The British, so often maligned about their Palestine policy, are sometimes accused of pursuing one of two ends, neither of which were among their calculations or would have brought them any advantage. The first suggestion is that they organized chaos in order that they might be invited to stay on. This is quickly disposed of. Had they wanted to stay, they would surely have jumped at the proposal for continuing trusteeship which the United States—alive at last to the danger of a fight—made on March 19, 1948. Instead, Mr. Bevin made it clear that the British were going, come what might:

"I do want to emphasize that we have to get into a position to enable us to be out of Palestine. That is the fundamental point of British policy."[48]

The second myth is that they organized chaos because they wanted a fight and wanted the Arabs to win it. This tale gained currency owing to some notable false prophecies (such as Field Marshal Montgomery's "The Jews have bought it") but it discounts the number of military authorities, notably Lord Wavell, who thought the opposite. Mr Attlee denied it as "utterly untrue"[49] and is to be believed because an Arab victory would have confronted the British government of 1948 with some unthinkable consequences. They would have been held accountable by the world for a new Jewish Dispersion, and for a victory won with the help of British officers serving with the Arab Legion. Not for an instant could they have entertained such disastrous consequences to their relations with the United States at a moment when every ounce of American goodwill was vital to them in Europe. For the summer of the Palestine war was also that of the Berlin crisis.

Certainly there were British Arabophiles who would have liked to see the Arab League repeat Saladin's feats, just as there were British Judeophiles who would have liked to see the Arabs move out as the Jews moved in, but neither had the last word in the making of British policy. But equally certainly, no one with responsibility of any kind for that policy expected the kind of Arab collapse that came about. What they expected, as they peered into the murk ahead, seems to have been the kind of sparring that had happened between Hindu and Moslem in the Punjab. When officials on the High Commissioner's

[48] House of Commons, March 23, 1948.
[49] House of Commons, January 26, 1949.

staff were asked by an enquiring correspondent what they expected would happen if, at the end, they simply locked their offices and dropped the key on the mat, the strongest word they tended to use was "*coup d'état*"—never "war".

It is inconceivable that a power of great overseas experience should have abandoned Palestine to chaos without some purpose for its action. The main motive was a purely British one—to save further loss of British life and to extract as much as possible of the very substantial amounts of British military material that had been transferred to Palestine; these were precious because of the risk of war over Berlin. A secondary motive was to bring the United Nations up against the practical problem of implementing its decision; as Mr Bevin said: "I wish other people would realize what enforcement meant before they voted so easily."[50] Another conception, which was to prevail, and with reason, all through 1948, was that the atmosphere in which western defence and oil interests must be preserved in the Middle East would be less unpromising if the Arabs were not totally humiliated.

The British attained their first objective. They succeeded well enough over the second, for both the United Nations Palestine Commission and the United States government were forced to admit during the spring of 1948 that the partition vote of the previous November could not be implemented without using troops. But they failed utterly in their third aim for two reasons. One was that they got no help from the Arabs. The other was that to reduce forces reduces power and influence; by April 1948, they had lost all control of events in Palestine, though they were so unaccustomed to powerlessness that they still behaved, and telegraphed instructions to their soldiers and ambassadors, as if they could shape events.

But this they could not do without using troops, and from mid-April onwards those troops were in a position to keep order only where doing so was compatible with getting out unscathed. Much Arab and Jewish ink has been spent on analysing how far this or that unit of the departing army favoured one side or other as it slipped out. But there was no intention to be partisan; the soldiers, bent on getting away with as little friction as possible, left the ground to whichever community was locally the better placed. Picture, for instance, a small and solitary Jewish outpost in the Safed area of Galilee; on April 15 it sees a British armoured column advancing along both the roads to its hideout; fearing cordon and arrest, it starts to conceal its arms, but, to its astonishment, the column trundles by; marvelling, it unearths its

[50] House of Commons, March 23, 1948.

arms again, but its numbers are too few to allow it to snatch the advantage, and Safed's strongpoints fall to the Arabs. Or take the famous case of Haifa: here the British commander, in a communication to the inhabitants of the town on April 21, exerts such authority as remains to him:

> "These clashes (between Jews and Arabs) must stop if law and order is to be preserved in Haifa."

But he is in no mind to stop them unless they actually interfere with British plans:

> "I have no desire whatsoever to involve my troops or members of the police in these clashes. All I want is to secure the routes and sectors that I need to complete the British evacuation of Palestine. . . ."[51]

But both Jews and Arabs, engrossed with their own concerns as anyone is at a moment of danger, could not credit his motives, and many still believe that it was he, and not the Jews, with their commanding military position and their superior arms and resolution, who engineered the Jewish capture of the town. At the moment of letting go, British tempers were at snapping-point, and, far away in London, Mr Bevin and Field Marshal Montgomery had their row over Haifa that the latter describes in his memoirs. But what can a departing army do the moment its instructions to get out unscathed start transcending its capacity to keep order anywhere except on its own thin line-of-march?

On paper, the best way to leave the Arabs with some cards in their hands was to induce them to accept partition and take over their share of the divided territory. In November the relevant British official had been told to prepare a scheme for devolution from central to local government which would have set the process in motion;[52] the instruction amounts to a last bid by the Colonial Office to salvage some of the good administrative machinery that it had built. But by spring all chance of this orderly procedure had vanished. In the evacuated parts of Palestine, Arab factions hostile to one another were fighting a series of single combats with the Jews. Outside it, Arab military preparations were proceeding with some flourishing of paper plans, and much distrust of King Abdullah, and without estimate of the strength of the Jewish adversary. At no Arab point, except in Transjordan, was there anyone to whom to hand over without making invidious choices

---

[51] Cf. "The Fall of Haifa" by Walid Khalidi, *Middle East Forum* (Beirut, December 1959).

[52] R. M. Graves, *Experiment in Anarchy* (London, 1949), p. 96.

between Arab rivals. To King Abdullah's prime minister, Mr Bevin personally recommended occupying the parts of the Arab share of the partition that were contiguous with Transjordan, "but do not go and invade the areas allotted to the Jews".[53] King Abdullah's was the only Arab government to follow this advice, and to recognize that it had not enough forces to do more. Bent on neutrality, the British decided that if there could be no handing over to the Arabs, there should be no handing over to the Jews.

After May 15, they were rid of the incubus of administrative responsibility which forever placed them in the position of doing something partisan; and they became free to act without inhibition in their own worldwide interests. Yet so long as their defence and oil interests constrained them to try and avoid acts that the Arabs could later bring up against them, their name for pro-Arab bias stuck; it did so not only among Zionists but among third parties—for example, servants of the United Nations.[54]

Certainly, bias coloured the thinking of some of the officials whose aim and duty it was to pursue British interests; the Foreign Office staff included not only missions in six major Arab capitals but a large complement of men with past experience in Arab countries who knew Arab hopes and fears in a way that they did not know those of the Jews. In the minds of many men whose jobs would become impossible were the Arabs to be totally mortified, national interest and private inclination coincided. But Mr Bevin's critics saw the private inclination only. A zenith of such feeling occurred at the moment in May 1948, when the White House was receiving the first president of Israel to discuss economic and political aid, and the British, though pressing for a cease-fire in Palestine, were falling in with the Arab request to postpone its application. It was at this juncture that the British cabinet went through one of its rare moments of disagreement, Sir Stafford Cripps in particular contending that Mr Bevin was not giving due weight to the importance of retaining American goodwill.[55]

Some of the acts that were ascribed to British favouring of the Arabs were unjustly so labelled. Some were wholly fortuitous, having their origins in arrangements that had nothing to do with Palestine. For instance, most of the Arab armies were British trained and got their arms from Britain, but this was an accident of Britain's own defence policy, not an anti-Jewish gesture. And the complement of British

---

[53] Glubb Pasha, *A Soldier with the Arabs* (London, 1957), pp. 63–6.

[54] Cf. Trygve Lie, *In the Cause of Peace* (New York, 1954), p. 164.

[55] *Ibid.*, p. 182; and Stewart Alsop in the *Washington Post*, June 7, 1948.

army officers serving with the Arab Legion had (as has already been explained) been strengthened in 1947 for British, not Arab purposes. Again, it was an accident, this time of geography, that the British Navy was able to head off vessels carrying Jewish immigrants of fighting age, whereas the British Army, once it had handed over control of the Jordan bridges to the Arab Legion, was unable to check reinforcements for the Arabs.

For less obvious reasons, Mr Bevin was misjudged over the Bernadotte Plan. This plan was put forward by the United Nations mediator, Count Bernadotte, on June 27—that is, during the first truce in Palestine, and three days before Mr Bevin and General Marshall announced that the western world was going to withstand the Soviet threat to besiege Berlin. Only when reading the diaries of the time is it possible to recapture the state of exhaustion to which the Berlin negotiations had reduced western statesmen. For months on end "an incident one way or other would have been like a match"[56] and Mr Bevin was haunted by the fear that "if the Russians are unsuccessful in their efforts in Berlin, they will immediately step up their efforts to exploit the chaos and disorder in the Middle East, if the U.S. and U.K. fail to stand firm. . . ."[57]

Both to him and to General Marshall, as they turned back to Palestine from discussions of more atomic bombers for British air-fields, or arrangements for re-establishing war-time controls, the Bernadotte Plan seemed satisfactory. It suited them because it was a stabilizer, providing for an accommodation between Israel and Jordan, and a link across the Negev between Egypt and the Arab states that might serve the oil interests of western Europe. Mr Bevin was also glad of the opportunity it gave of getting back into line with the Americans, while General Marshall liked its implication that the U.N. partition plan "was not completely rigid".[58] Up to October, the State Department was asking for forces to help the Mediator implement it. But the Israelis hated it because, though it gave them all Galilee, it gave Jerusalem and most of the Negev to the Arabs. In their antagonism to it, they omitted to notice that in welcoming it Mr Bevin had for the first time officially accepted partition.

Its defeat by the White House, for reasons of American internal politics, less than a month before the presidential election of 1948, is

[56] To the Labour Party Conference, Margate, October 5, 1950.
[57] U.S. Embassy report to the State Department from London, quoted in *The Forrestal Diaries*, p. 441.
[58] H. S. Truman, *Memoirs*, Vol. II, p. 167.

described with naïveté by President Truman when he explains why and how it "had become necessary" for him to declare that the Negev must be Jewish and make the statement which he and General Marshall "had earlier agreed not to make".[59] A scheme favoured by the Foreign Secretary and Secretary of State as being for the general good of the west was thus metamorphosed into another British trap from which President Truman had delivered Israel.

But there were incidents in which the argument that Britain was promoting only its own interests is weak. An example is the refusal, so long as fighting which had ceased to be Britain's individual business continued, to release Jews of military age from the Cyprus camps; up till at least December 1947, the intention had been to clear these before the end of the mandate;[60] the idea was not dropped until the communities came to blows. Another is British support for a series of U.N. resolutions that sought to curb the Israelis' wish to claim both their military gains in Arab areas, and the award of unconquered areas allotted to them in the original partition scheme. Even Mr Bevin's admirers have to acknowledge that his policy had entailed withstanding, in the spring, U.N. resolutions that were unpopular with the Arabs while supporting, in the autumn, U.N. resolutions that were unpopular with the Jews.

The climax of Mr Bevin's reputation for bias occurred in the first days of 1949 over an incident for which he bore no individual responsibility, but which critics of his personal bias lay at his door. In southern Palestine the victorious Israelis crossed the Egyptian frontier. The Jordanians invoked their treaty with Britain, and British troops were landed at Aqaba. The Egyptians, for obvious reasons, refused to invoke the Anglo-Egyptian treaty; indeed, they asked that news of the frontier violations should be kept quiet, for they had long been deluding their public with false bulletins. How far were the Israelis going? The British forces on the Suez Canal were by habit sensitive about keeping other people's little wars away from this artery, and the British Chiefs of Staff ordered air reconnaissance. It was an expedition of a kind they had been in the habit of flying without notice when they were paramount, and which, apparently, they had continued to fly throughout 1948. All such sorties were flown "on government authority" but the sanction was a blanket one, and the timing was in the hands of the Air Officer Commanding in the Canal Zone. Mr Attlee, when under pressure by questioners in the House of Commons,

[59] H. S. Truman, *Memoirs*, Vol. II, p. 168.
[60] Mr Bevin, House of Commons, December 12, 1947.

therefore felt justified in denying that "these reconnaissances were ordered by this government".[61] But during that flown on January 7, the Israelis shot down four Spitfires, and Mr Bevin—at Mr Crossman's hands both in the press and in Parliament—was held to blame for an incident which caused the government majority to fall from 177 to 100.[62]

But it is an exaggeration to suggest, as some do, that this revolt of about 70 members of the Labour Party against an attitude of which the public had grown weary was the sole cause of its sequel—the release of the Jews from Cyprus and the recognition of Israel. The following date sequence suggests that these events would have happened anyway: on January 7 the Egyptians asked for a cease-fire; on the 13th, the armistice talks opened in Rhodes; on the 18th the Cyprus camp inmates were released; on the 19th, Israel held its first elections; on the 29th, it was recognized *de facto* as being a state with an established government by Great Britain in conjunction with all its Brussels Treaty colleagues and along with a score of other nations. Before condemning Mr Bevin's acts as unmatchedly peculiar, it is well to remember the peculiarity of American and Soviet recognition, in May 1948, of a state that had neither of two usual American requirements—a government supported by "the will of the people constitutionally declared" and free within its boundaries from "active resistance to its rule".[63]

Great Britain suffered mortification over the undignified end of its mandate for Palestine, and Mr Bevin personified this. Often during the remaining two years of his life he revealed how much he took it to heart by making long analyses of what would have happened "if they had listened to me". By his standards, any human problem was soluble; he never grumbled about the impossible shape in which the Palestine one had reached his hands.

But Palestine had for some time before the end ceased to be a British

[61] House of Commons, January 26, 1949; cf. the circumstances in which President Eisenhower on May 5, 1960, denied all knowledge of a reconnaissance flight by an American U2 high-altitude aircraft shot down over the Soviet Union —a denial which, said Mr Khrushchev, "made matters even worse because it showed that the militarists and generals were in actual power", *The Observer*, May 8, 1960.

[62] "I accuse Bevin", editorial headline to a message from R. H. S. Crossman, then in Israel, to the *Sunday Pictorial*, January 16, 1949; and House of Commons debate, January 26, 1949.

[63] L. Oppenheim, *International Law: a Treatise*, edited by H. Lauterpacht (1948), Vol. I, chap. I, para. 73c.

interest of importance. Chagrin over it was soon dwarfed by more vital preoccupations—notably by the developments in western Europe that are probably the greatest creative political achievements of our time—O.E.E.C. and N.A.T.O. Simultaneously, worry had set in over China. The American White Paper that wrote off Chiang Kai-shek as an ally and conceded communist victory there was published on August 5, 1949.[64] The spread of American anxiety into the Middle East was made plain in the Tripartite Declaration of May 25, 1950 (that is, issued a month before war broke out in Korea), which sought to freeze the frontier and armaments situation in Palestine.

Set against changes of this magnitude, the establishment of British relations with Israel was an act to be taken in Mr Bevin's stride, and it was so. He instructed his first ambassador—Sir Knox Helm—to induce the Israelis to forget the past; he gave him pride of place at the conference of Middle East ambassadors in the summer of 1949, which Helm perforce attended in a minority of one. His private attempts to re-establish peace between Jew and Arab were sufficiently memorable to be recalled, ten years later, in a farewell interview which the retiring Israel ambassador, Mr Eliahu Elath, gave on leaving England in 1959.[65]

Relations with the Arabs grew no better for the efforts he had made to save them from an abyss. His short interlude of "Arab policy" had been pro-Arab only to non-Arabs; by Arab standards it had accomplished nothing. The end of the fighting left most Arabs and Egyptians stunned, resentful of their own leaders, and without any powerful foreign friend to whom to turn. If Mr Bevin had hoped to win from them a rating as less obnoxious than the unpredictable Russians or the pro-Zionist Americans, his hope was vain; it was fulfilled only within the orbits of confirmed anglophiles such as King Abdullah and Nuri Pasha, and lasted only as long as they did. In the end it vanished everywhere, beginning in Egypt and ending in Iraq, killed by the exigencies of Britain's own defence policy.

Some events of Mr Bevin's last full year of office, which was 1950, sum up the impossibility of fulfilling his aims in the Arab world as it was. In January 1950, he paid his only visit to Egypt. He was ill with the heart trouble that killed him, so that he gave some of the Egyptians whom he met the impression that he had not the stamina to say much, yet had something urgent to say. To their surprise, this was not a harangue on defending the Suez Canal, but on bettering the fellahin. He was on his way back from the Colombo Conference which he had

[64] Department of State Publication 3573; Far Eastern Series 30.
[65] The Observer, September 27, 1959.

insisted on attending, and his mind was full of his prime interest, which was improving the lot of people who had had a bad start in life. He knew the ropes,[66] and would have had much in common with the plotting army officers whom he did not meet in Cairo.

But 1950 was the year of the Korean war. By May he was asking that the British Chief of the Imperial General Staff should call in Cairo on his way East, and pave the way to new treaty talks. The Egyptian Green Book on the conversations of 1950–51[67] (which is, with its many verbatim records, a fuller and more revealing document than the matching British White Paper)[68] is a monument to the impossibility of conducting an Arab policy so long as Britain wanted military privileges in Arab territory. It reveals how high was the barrier constituted by legacies of the past; by the antithesis between the Egyptian wish to be trusted and a brew of familiarity and disdain which the British reserved for the Egyptians; and by the total lack of a common denominator between a parochial power owning a strategic key-point, and a worldwide power lacking both the will to seize control of this and the means to cajole it:

> "Your foreign policy is of such a wide range that it almost embraces all international problems", said Salah al-Din Bey, Egypt's Foreign Minister, during almost his last talk with Mr Bevin. "But our foreign policy is a very limited one, and can almost be resolved in these two questions now under discussion, the question of evacuation and that of the unity of Egypt and the Sudan under the Egyptian crown."[69]

The grievance against the British over Palestine came first with homeless Palestinians, or with Syrians who had forgotten the fact of foreign occupation, but to Egyptians the real rub was British military policy and the slur of "incomplete sovereignty".[70]

At the beginning of Mr Bevin's term of office, his diplomatic inclinations towards the Arab world had been thwarted by the post-war confusion, by Britain's penury and by mistrust of Soviet plans. At the end, some of these curbs were less drastic, but some remained. He

---

[66] Cf. Alan Bullock, *The Life and Times of Ernest Bevin* (London, 1960), chap. I.
[67] Cairo, Ministry of Foreign Affairs, 1951.
[68] Cmd. 8419.
[69] December 9, 1950. *Egyptian Green Book*, pp. 95–6.
[70] Nahas Pasha to Field Marshal Sir William Slim, June 5, 1950. *Egyptian Green Book*, p. 13. Most Egyptian books of the period put the grievances in this order of importance: cf. Anwar Sadat, *Revolt on the Nile* (London, 1957), p. 103.

liked Arabs, but his approach to them was defeated, first in Egypt and after his death elsewhere, by the combined weight of old British traditions and new British anxieties.

He died in April 1951, three months before King Abdullah was murdered and some years before the Foreign Office added Arab neutralism to the list of its perplexities.

© ELIZABETH MONROE 1961

A DECADE OF DISCOVERY:
AMERICA IN THE MIDDLE EAST, 1947–1958

By William R. Polk

HARSH WORDS for the conduct of American foreign relations in the Middle East have become common in recent years. Few writers, other than officials, have found many encouraging comments to make. Some of the criticism has been irresponsible or ill-informed, yet enough has been written to indicate that many able and experienced students of our international relations believe that the United States Government has often acted in haste, in response to the prior actions of others, frequently without regard to the desires and fears of those who live in the Middle East, and consequently has seldom achieved its announced goals.

The most basic criticism of American actions in the Middle East is that they do not constitute an American Middle Eastern policy. In Europe the United States developed the two policies of containment and economic assistance. These it has applied with varying success to the Far East, South America, and, as will be shown, to the Middle East. Always the object of American policy has been the Soviet Union. It is not surprising that this should be so. But the question raised by the complex strains of the events of recent years is whether or not an anti-Russian policy constitutes a Middle Eastern policy, capable of giving some sort of coherence to American acts there.

The following is a brief account of American involvement in the Middle East prior to 1947 when the United States began large-scale activities there; then in more detail the events since 1947 are traced along with American attempts to formulate reactions to them; finally an analysis of the unfolding of American programmes and the effects of American endeavour is offered.[1]

* * *

[1] This paper is a history of the development of American policy, and does not attempt to deal with the question of what American policy *should* be. The question is posed, and an attempt made to answer it, by R. H. Nolte and W. R. Polk, in "Towards a Policy for the Middle East" in *Foreign Affairs*, July 1958.

Unlike other areas of the world, notably the Far East, the Middle East held few lures for Americans in the nineteenth and early twentieth centuries. Almost the sole exception was the American missionary for whom the Land of the Bible was unmatchable. But if the early missionary found it attractive, he also found its people so ignorant of their heritage and so bound down by the ills of this world as to be unwilling and unable to aspire to a higher calling. So, starting in 1831, small bands of American missionaries began laying the foundations of what by the end of the century had grown into a network of schools, colleges and hospitals in Syria, Anatolia, and Egypt. For the most part, the Americans were sustained, in times of crisis, by British consular efforts. Rarely was much notice taken of them by the United States Government except that it frequently augmented its own small diplomatic corps by appointing missionaries as part-time consuls.

American trade with the Middle East was on a small scale since few of the area's products were needed by America. When Americans went east, they went mainly to the Far East which was usually of easier access to them, and, of course, was accessible not through any of the traditional European routes, including the Euphrates or the Red Sea, but directly westward across the Pacific. It was not until the discovery of oil in the Middle East that this picture changed.

In short, prior to the end of the First World War, American interests in the area were largely those of protecting the few American citizens resident there when it was inconvenient or impractical for Great Britain to do this.

President Wilson's declarations on self-determination led to a belief, on the part of many more directly interested in Middle Eastern affairs than were Americans, that the United States would accept a large measure of responsibility for the achievement of a just and enduring peace, based upon the applications of its own domestic political ideals, in the Middle East. There was a period in which it seemed to be moving in this direction, as in the Armenian question. American suspicions of the intentions of Britain and France caused the United States Government to send to the Middle East the King-Crane Commission to ascertain the desires of the native population. At the Peace Conference, an American Zionist delegation persuaded President Wilson to urge the application of the Balfour Declaration. But in the return to isolationism, these efforts amounted to little. A bill urging an American protectorate for Armenia was killed in Congress; the report of the King-Crane Commission was probably never seen by Wilson and was not published in the United States until the end of 1922, and while the

American Congress passed the first of several resolutions approving the Balfour Declaration, it was unprepared to do much to realize its terms.

The return to isolationalism was not, however, complete. Oil interests, grown strong already within America, were pressing for free entry into the new and promising field of the Middle East while their British, Dutch, and French competitors were anxious to keep these areas to themselves. In this case, for the first time, the American State Department took an active part in securing American access to the area. But the chief motivation behind the United States action, fear that its own reserves were near exhaustion, was weakened by successive petroleum discoveries on the North American continent. Consequently, having achieved its purpose, the United States Government took little further part in Middle Eastern affairs until the coming of World War II.

During World War II, with the notable exceptions of stimulating Saudi Arabian oil production and establishing of the Persian Gulf–Iran route to Russia, America took a decidedly secondary role in Middle Eastern activities; the area was British, and the United States was content that it be such. Where useful, the United States could associate herself with Great Britain, as in the Middle East Supply Centre or in the moves to evict France from Lebanon and Syria, but the United States was, as it traditionally had been, far more concerned with other areas.

At the end of the war, the United States Government resisted British attempts to draw it into a responsible position in Middle Eastern politics. With its own overseas might in a period of severe contraction, its deep sense of involvement in the Far East and Germany, its people's desire to return to their homes to enjoy the fruits of wartime prosperity, was joined the conviction that Great Britain had both the power and the experience to handle the problems of the Middle East. Few in 1945 thought otherwise. Thus, while President Truman on April 6, 1946, spoke in strong terms about the area's weakness and instability, and its importance to the West, he was willing only to work through the United Nations, as in the Iranian dispute, or to offer mediation as through the Anglo-American Committee of Inquiry in Palestine, but not to accept responsibility.

This situation was drastically changed when, in February 1947, it was publicly announced that Great Britain was no longer able to sustain its commitments in Greece and Turkey.

It will be recalled that the U.S.S.R. had refused to participate in the

supervision of elections in Greece in 1946 and that the Greek Communist Party was the leader of the rebel group in the civil war. Soviet
territorial demands upon Turkey in 1945 and the prolonged stay of
Russian troops in Iran into 1946, emphasized as these were by events
in the Balkans, convinced the American government, particularly
Secretary Forrestal, that America must counter Soviet pressure, that
whatever the causes of the Greek revolt, Greece must not be allowed to
fall into the Soviet camp. This has been termed Mr Churchill's contribution to American thinking on south Europe. The United States
Government's answer to this challenge was a pragmatic one: it should
give that which it could easily, money, withholding that which was
difficult for it, men. This was the essence of the Truman Doctrine
which grew out of the President's statement before Congress on March
12, 1947:

> "The United States has received from the Greek Government an
> urgent appeal for financial and economic assistance . . . assistance is
> imperative if Greece is to survive as a free nation. . . . There is no
> other country to which democratic Greece can turn [as] the British
> Government, which has been helping Greece, can give no further
> financial or economic aid after March 31. Great Britain finds itself
> under the necessity of reducing or liquidating its commitments in
> several parts of the world, including Greece.
>
> " . . . If Greece should fall under the control of an armed minority,
> the effect upon its neighbor, Turkey, would be immediate and
> serious. Confusion and disorder might well spread throughout the
> entire Middle East."[2]

The President went on to say that the United States had contributed
341 billion dollars toward winning World War II and "It is only
common sense that we should safeguard this investment and make sure
that it was not in vain".

It was at this point, then, that America undertook the first direct and
large-scale responsibility for events in the eastern Mediterranean. It
did so in default of Great Britain, to whom it had preferred to leave
responsibility for the area. And through its European commitments
in Greece, America eased into an involvement in the Middle East.

The importance of Greece in the development of American policy is
twofold. On the one hand, it was the first step in filling what had come
to be thought of as a power vacuum. On the other, Greece provided a

[2] Unless otherwise noted, all quotations are drawn from the Department of
State *Bulletin*.

key precedent for all future American action. This latter is so crucial to any study of American post-war thought as to deserve our close attention.

In the American analysis, the allotment of American credits and the sending of American technical personnel, both civilian and military, was the formula by which Greece was saved from Communism. These two factors have been emphasized almost to the exclusion of all others in the Greek situation. There is certainly much truth in this analysis. The recovery of Greece was unlikely without American aid and the scale upon which that aid was given, nearly $2 billion from July 1945 to June 1952, tremendously accelerated the pace of recovery. It seems likely also that the training and direction given in the spending of this money, despite much valid criticism which was or could have been directed at the details of the programme, made the money more wisely distributed than otherwise would have been likely. But that other factors were also vital is a fact which cannot seriously be denied. It would, for example, be hard to deny that Tito's break from the Cominform, with the ensuing split within the ranks of the Greek guerrilla movement, played a crucial role in the victory of the Greek Government. A detailed study of the timetable of the civil war might, indeed, indicate that American measures played a lesser role in that victory. However, in disregard of the special features of the Greek situation, the American measures adopted there were widely looked upon as the sure formula of success, and Greece became a model of the way in which crises could and should be handled.

For all the concentration and intensity of interest which it has evoked, the Palestine problem was long in calling forth such a clear expression of official American policy. The reasons are basically three. In the first place, the Palestine problem has involved, more than any other of the overseas endeavours of the United States, an extension of domestic American politics. Both the Jewish Zionists, with well-directed, large-scale campaigns to influence the American public, and American liberals, shocked and outraged by the brutality of the Nazis and fearful of the future of anti-Semitism in Europe and America, have made the issue of the settlement of Jews in Israel their own affair. In the second place, in the growing concern with the Soviet Union, the problem of Palestine seemed to challenge no basic and vital American interest; whereas the United States Government was not prepared to allow Greece or Turkey to slip out of control, it was prepared, within limits, to allow hostilities in Palestine. In the third place, the Palestine issue, as it still faces the world, may be said to have been fixed at a time when the United States was not responsibly engaged in the Middle East. To this writer, it seems that the Palestine problem was complete in all but the amplification of details by 1920, and certainly these had been added by the end of World War II. The United States, coming to the problem at that time, could not but feel a lack of desire to assume responsibility for the settling of a problem which had not been of its creation. What the United States did was not, however, blameless. From the safety of its detached position it urged Britain to action or decision, to admit increasingly large numbers of Jewish refugees to Palestine, yet to protect the rights of the Arab community. The quest of the so-called "Jewish vote" led to politicking on the highest levels of the Democratic and Republican parties, to the by-passing of the State Department in the control of international acts, and finally to a series of pathetically contradictory moves. With much justice, this has been characterized by J. C. Hurewitz as "irresolution, irresponsibility, and indifference".

When Great Britain indicated that she was unable to resolve the conflict and intended to wash her hands of the problem, by turning it over to the United Nations, the United States played a major role in pushing through the General Assembly, in November 1947, a modification of the latest partition plan which had been devised by U.N.S.C.O.P. However, the United States Government felt unable to lend the U.N. the force which might have made partition possible without war. The military establishment was depleted, and those planning American policy could not count on Congressional or party support. Unable to move forward with any confidence, the Government on March 19 suggested at the U.N. that action on partition be suspended and that a trusteeship be established over all Palestine to delay final settlement. When this was refused, both by the U.S.S.R. and by Great Britain, the United States swung back into a strong position on partition and recognized the State of Israel within minutes after it was proclaimed. Meanwhile, at the U.N., the United States urged the creation of the U.N. Palestine Conciliation Commission. When the latter was established in December 1948, the United States undertook its first direct responsibility by serving as a member (along with France and Turkey). To support and, hopefully, to resettle the Arab refugees, the United States co-operated in the formation, and has subsequently paid most of the expenses, of the U.N. Relief for Palestine Refugees (U.N.R.P.R.) and Relief and Works Agency (U.N.R.W.A.).

Outside of the United Nations, the United States joined Britain and France in issuing the May 25, 1950, Tripartite Declaration on the security of Middle Eastern frontiers, out of "the desire to promote the establishment and maintenance of peace and stability in the area and their unalterable opposition to the use of force or threat of force between any of the states in that area". This undertaking was subsequently reconfirmed by Secretary Dulles when he returned from his inspection trip to the Middle East in May of 1953. In the Middle East, Secretary Dulles said he had ascertained that the Arabs were "more fearful of Zionism than of the Communists" because they thought that "the United States will back the new State of Israel in aggressive expansion". A new situation within the United States Government was suggested by the statement that the United States would "seek to allay the deep resentment against it that has resulted from the creation of Israel". Such soon was shown to be the case.

Israel at this point of her statehood was dependent upon American governmental and private aid. The latter was pouring into Israel in loans and U.S. income-tax deductible gifts at the rate of about $50 million yearly. In the fiscal year 1953, American aid still accounted for an estimated 35 per cent of the imports into Israel. The new administration saw this factor as one of considerable leverage in influencing Israeli policy and used it as the previous administration had not.

When, in the early summer of 1953, the Israeli Government began to move its offices to Jerusalem from Tel Aviv, the United States Government protested that this violated the 1947 U.N. Partition resolution making Jerusalem into an international city. Shortly thereafter, the U.N. Truce Supervision Organization, acting on a Syrian protest, requested that Israel not undertake a hydro-electric project on the Jordan River at Banat Yaqub, but Israel in September refused to halt work. On October 14–15, the Israeli army raided the village of Qibiya and killed 53 Arabs. Joined by France and Great Britain, the United States brought this issue to the Security Council, and Secretary Dulles, noting that the United States had "played an essential part in creating the State of Israel", admonished Israel that "this was clearly an occasion to invoke the concept of decent respect for the opinion of mankind as represented by the United Nations". At the same time, it was announced that since September 25 the United States had been withholding an allocation of Mutual Security Funds because Israel was acting in defiance of the U.N. On October 27, Israel suspended work in the demilitarized zone, and the next day Secretary Dulles recommended a grant of $26,250,000 in economic aid for that fiscal year.

This direct linking of economic aid to compliance with American wishes was the beginning of a policy which was subsequently, in the Eisenhower Doctrine, to be carried a step further but which was at that time contradictory to assurances given that American economic aid was "without strings".

Plain speaking on the Palestine issue drew hostile comments from both Israel and the Arab States. Assistant Secretary Byroade in particular was criticized for setting out American policy in 1957 in the following terms:

> "To the Israelis, I say that you should come to truly look upon yourselves as a Middle Eastern state and see your own future in that context rather than as a headquarters, or nucleus so to speak, or world-wide groupings of peoples or a particular religious faith who must have special rights within and obligations to the Israeli state. You should drop the attitude of a conqueror and the conviction that force and a policy of retaliatory killings is the only policy that your neighbors will understand. You should make your deeds correspond to your frequent utterances of the desire for peace.
>
> "To the Arabs I say you should accept this state of Israel as an accomplished fact. I say further that you are deliberately attempting to maintain a state of affairs delicately suspended between peace and war, while at present desiring neither. This is a most dangerous policy and one which world opinion will increasingly condemn if you continue to resist any move to obtain at least a less dangerous *modus vivendi* with your neighbor."

Border tension continued to increase with raids on the one side and on the other the announcement and fulfilment of Israel's policy of retaliation. The February 28, 1955, attack on Gaza was the high point of these clashes; for it, the Security Council censured Israel on March 29. But since the Gaza raid may be taken as the key event in the build-up to the Czech arms deal, it will be useful at this point to leave the Palestine problem to return to a second sequence of moves, the attempt by the United States Government to improve the economies of the Middle Eastern states.

The American experiment with "pump priming" under the New Deal was perhaps the most extensive governmental economic endeavour in our experience. Its basic idea was the reallocation of wealth both between our several states and between social groups. It was, of course, the policy of the Democratic party, but Republican hostility toward it had been muted by time to the point that a number of influential Republicans, of whom some were men of vast personal wealth, had accepted the utility or inevitability of governmental economic stimulation. Wartime spending accustomed the public to large outlays by the Government of funds and the use of these funds for the creation of new industries. It seems quite natural in this context that in 1947 the United States Government should propose the Marshall Plan for European Recovery. "It is logical," said Secretary Marshall,

"that the United States should do whatever it is able to do to assist in the return of normal economic health in the world, without which there can be no political stability and no assured peace. Our policy is directed not against any country or doctrine but against hunger, poverty, desperation, and chaos. Its purpose should be the revival of a working economy in the world so as to permit the emergence of political and social conditions in which free institutions can exist."

The basic ideas contained in the Secretary's address were elaborated and carried a logical step forward in the famous Fourth Point of President Truman's inaugural address in 1949:

"We must embark on a bold new program for making the benefits of our scientific advances and industrial progress available for the improvement and growth of underdeveloped areas. . . . Our aim should be to help the free peoples of the world, through their own efforts, to produce more food, more clothing, more materials for housing, and more mechanical power to lighten their burdens."

Bold the Point IV programme was in many ways but new it was essentially not. In a sense it was closer to the main stream of American overseas activity than was the Marshall Plan, which was an emergency measure to restore rather than to create. Point IV was right in line with a series of previous American endeavours, beginning in 1935 with the Export-Import Bank which had loaned over $700 million to Latin American states by the time Point IV was created. At the end of the war, the International Bank and the International Monetary Fund had been created, largely on the initiative of the United States. The exchange of personnel programme was extended to the Middle East in 1943 by President Roosevelt and the United States took an active, though secondary, role in the Middle East Supply Centre's work in Cairo; the Fulbright Act was passed in 1946, and between 1945 and 1950 Export-Import Bank Loans totalled $266,110,000 to Middle Eastern and Asian States. Also the United States had already undertaken a share in the responsibility for the Palestine refugees' economic future through the U.N.R.P.R.

A logical outgrowth of the latter programme was the notion that the Arab refugees could not be permanently supported on an international dole and that measures of an investment nature would have to be undertaken to reintegrate them into the economy of the Middle East. To this end, the State Department urged the U.N. Conciliation Commission for Palestine to send to the Middle East an economic survey mission under the leadership of Gordon R. Clapp, the chairman of the board of the Tennessee Valley Authority. Out of the Clapp Commission report came the establishment of the U.N. Relief and Works Agency and, not less important, a broad scheme for the economic development of the whole area due to the recognition that "solution of the problem of poverty and unemployment of the refugees is ... inseparable from a solution of the problem of poverty and hunger as that already affects a large section of the population of the Middle East".

The United States Government undertook to assist in both of these aspects. The United States contributed $45 million to the initial U.N. Palestine Refugee work and yearly since has met over one-half of the budget of U.N.R.W.A. The 1950 Act for International Development set aside $34·5 million for technical assistance while the 1951 Mutual Security Appropriation Act set up a $160 million fund for technical and economic assistance and $21·5 million for general Point IV aid. In addition the United States contributed $12 million to the U.N. technical assistance programme for the 18 months from July 1, 1950. In the following years, these amounts have been generally increased so that by the end of the fiscal year 1957, the United States had advanced some $1,145,500,000 worth of economic and technical assistance to the countries of the Middle East.

In presenting the argument for the Mutual Security Programme for the fiscal year beginning July 1, 1952, the Administration gave an appraisal of the problems of the area which has been little affected by the change of administration:

"Political unrest and intense nationalism characterize many of the countries in this area, and in part reflect deep-rooted social and economic ills.... The poverty resulting from these factors [*viz.* inefficient and unscientific land and water use techniques, untrained and inefficient labor force, antiquated feudal land-tenure systems, and inadequately developed land and water resource base, and a lack of capital for investment] together with a disease and illiteracy contributing to them, form a vicious circle which we can help to break by the application of technical skills."

Given this analysis, the policy of the United States was to

". . . assist the people and governments of the area to achieve not only greater military security, through the Middle East Command and limited military assistance, but also to assist responsible leaders in getting under way orderly reform and development, in which the energies of the people can find constructive expansion. Our purpose is to demonstrate to these countries, by concrete cooperative effort, that they themselves can achieve their desires for economic and social progress as a part of the free world. People who have evidence of this will not turn in desperation to Communism."

Initial reception in the area was good: Israel, Libya, Egypt, Saudi Arabia, Lebanon, Jordan and, subsequently, Iraq entered into Point IV or subsequent aid agreements. Nearly 700 American technicians were involved in projects throughout the area and Secretary Acheson summed up the hope and assumption of the whole programme as "encouraging the growth of free institutions through which peoples can develop their respective cultures and ways of life". In the early days of the programme, this hope went unquestioned.

The change of administration brought no drastic changes in American policy; the Middle East was not mentioned in President Eisenhower's Inaugural Address in January of 1953. However, the new Secretary of State, John Foster Dulles, announced that he would go on the first of his many, wide-ranging trips to trouble spots for a personal look at the Middle East. Upon his return on May 29 from twenty days in the area Mr Dulles indicated the new shift he wanted to make toward Asian affairs by saying simply, "It is high time that the United States Government paid more attention to the Near East and South Asia." But under the impact of the Korean War, American thinking increasingly followed military paths in its quest for security, and American funds were forthcoming mainly for military projects. To these we will now turn.

From the period following the Palestine war, American aid may be seen as one means of diverting Middle Eastern energies and attention both from intra-area hostility and from the lure of Communism. American policy planners never changed in their close attention to what they regarded as the overriding goal of our policy, to counter or contain the Soviet Union. The policy of containment, set out in its original form by Ambassador George Kennan as Mr X in *Foreign Affairs* in 1947, had been closely linked with economic aid. In the Mutual Security Programme recommended to Congress by President Truman on May 24, 1951, the union of these concepts was clearly spelled out. Aid to the Middle East was necessary, said President Truman, because the Soviet Union was applying to the area "steady and relentless pressure" which the area was unable, alone, to withstand,

" . . . endangered by political and economic instability; the security objective in the area must be to create stability by laying solid foundations, now, of economic progress and by establishing, now, confidence that further advances can be made."

But, increasingly, money allocated was to be put directly into military strength rather than into programmes to build economic strength. Of the $540 million proposed for the Middle East, exclusive of economic assistance given to Greece and Turkey, $415 million was to be spent on military aid, mainly for Greece, Turkey, and Iran. (In authorizing the funds, Congress decreased the military allotment to $396,250,000 and increased the non-military budget.) Even at this date the Government was clearly most concerned with the military aspects of what Secretary Dulles was later to call the "northern tier of nations" and in September and October invited Turkey and Greece to make arrangements to join in the military planning work of N.A.T.O. Both accepted and in the following September were invited to join as full members.

The rest of the Middle East presented a pact-maker's nightmare. Iran, already in serious financial troubles, was involved in its dispute with A.I.O.C. and the British Government and thus was a most unlikely partner in a British-led pact. (The United States clearly thought until the Suez crisis that any military group in the Middle East should be led by Great Britain.) Israel was an unlikely choice since its participation would automatically exclude the Arab states. The centre of military strength at that time was at Suez and in British thinking Egypt was the pivot of Middle Eastern power. Therefore, Egypt seemed to be the logical place to start. Consequently, on October 13, 1951, Great Britain, France, Turkey, and the United States invited Egypt to help found the Allied Middle East Command. If Egypt were prepared to join and to agree to the use of her facilities, including the Suez base, a political plum of considerable psychological value was to be given in return: Great Britain would agree to suppress the Anglo-Egyptian treaty of 1936 and would withdraw all British forces not assigned to the Command. It was also made clear, however, that Egypt's demands on the Sudan would not be met.

Given the political climate in Egypt, no worse formula nor any worse time could have been chosen. Prime Minister Nahhas's government was weak and shot through with domestic corruption which it was attempting to hide in safe patriotism. It was publicly committed to the "Unity of the Nile Valley" and could hardly have been willing to give its domestic enemies the weapon they could have fashioned from Wafd acceptance of continued British presence under such a transparent label. Nahhas clearly had to reject the proposal decisively and this he did within two days; the Egyptian Parliament also subsequently voted unanimously to reject, unilaterally, the 1936 treaty under which British troops were then in Suez. Thus, not only did the West not get a better co-ordinated defence arrangement but it seriously weakened its existing operation. Further complications arose from the refusal of both the British and American Governments to face the realities of the Egyptian situation. With more legal justification than political utility, Secretary Acheson issued the following statement:

> "The United States Government must reaffirm its belief that the action of the Egyptian government with respect to the Anglo-Egyptian treaty of 1936 and the agreements of 1899 regarding the Sudan is not in accord with proper respect for international obligations. For its part, the United States Government considers the action of the Egyptian Government to be without validity."

The United States Government was not prepared to give up. Despite the Egyptian rejection and Soviet protests that the United States was trying to draw the Middle East into the "aggressive Atlantic bloc", the United States Government tried to keep the project alive, maintaining that Egypt had not "understood" the plan and that a proper understanding would win its support to a programme of such obvious utility. The visit of Prime Minister Churchill to the United States in January of 1952 strengthened the feeling in Washington that the withdrawal of British power in the Middle East would necessitate some form of regional association to safeguard the area. This continued to be the desire of the American Government until the May 1953 visit of Secretary Dulles to the Middle East.

Returning from that trip, Mr Dulles indicated that he had come to the conclusion that it was not then feasible to attempt to create a

Middle East parallel to N.A.T.O. There was, he found, "a vague desire to have a collective security system, but no such system can be imposed from without. It should be designed and grow from within out of a sense of common destiny and common danger." No two senses could be further from the thoughts—and nerves—of the Arab states, where, as mentioned above, Mr Dulles found that American fear of Communism was paralleled by Arab fear of Israel. But elsewhere Mr Dulles found hope. "However, there is more concern where the Soviet Union is near. In general the northern tier of nations shows awareness of this [Soviet-Communist] danger." The implications of this finding represented less of a new departure in American action, which had throughout the period contributed heavily to Greece, Turkey, and Iran, than a departure from the ideal strategic model of the British, based upon Suez, a plan, incidentally, upon which the Arab League Collective Security Pact had been partly based.

Renewed Soviet pressure upon Turkey, again relating to the Turkish Straits, strengthened Secretary Dulles's emphasis on the areas adjacent to the Soviet Union, the "northern tier", and the United States made haste to inform these states that they could have aid for the asking. Under the Mutual Security Act signed July 16, 1953, Greece, Turkey, and Iran were granted $396,250,000 in military aid.

Extension of the "northern tier" concept into the Baghdad Pact was a development in which the United States Government took the keenest interest without playing an overt part. It was thought in Washington that however much use of the carrot and the stick were required, the states involved must pull or at least seem to pull their own loads. By late in 1953, the United States had begun to plan a military assistance agreement with Pakistan which materialized in May 1954; on April 2, 1954, Turkey and Pakistan signed a military pact. When Pakistan joined the South-east Asia Collective Defence Treaty in September, it became obvious that in the making was a belt of defence treaties from Europe to the Far East. The United States extended military assistance to Iraq in April of 1954. In February 1955 Turkey and Iraq signed the Mutual Co-operation Pact which was opened to all members of the Arab League and other states concerned with peace and security in the Middle East. The United Kingdom adhered to this agreement on April 4 and terminated the Anglo-Iraqi treaty of 1930; Pakistan joined September 23 and Iran on October 11.

This by-passing of the Arab League Pact and basing of the new pact upon Baghdad led to a steady deterioration of relations with the other Arab states, particularly those in which President Nasser had strong influence, first Syria, then Saudi Arabia, and for a time Jordan. This development, coupled with the growing tensions along the Arab-Israeli frontier and probably with internal pressures in the Egyptian army, caused Nasser to conclude the arms purchase agreement with Czechoslovakia.

The really surprising feature of the Czech arms deal is that it did not come earlier. Supply of arms had been a cardinal feature of American policy since the end of World War II; the United States Government was clearly of the opinion that the acquisition of arms was not wrong. Moreover, when, in the Palestine war, Israel had sought for and received arms also from Czechoslovakia, the United States had not objected. The United States had itself offered arms to Egypt shortly before the Czech deal but upon terms which Egypt would not accept. Expression of concern was quick to come, however, when the United States learned in August of 1955 that the Soviet Union had offered arms apparently on a large scale. President Nasser announced the arrangement on September 27, and on September 28 Ambassador George Allen was sent to Cairo on a special mission, presumably to reactivate and make more acceptable the earlier American arms offer. If this interpretation of the situation is true, and it seems likely, then the American response to the Russian move set what President Nasser was to regard subsequently as a precedent—the key to American motivations—when he came to negotiate aid for the Aswan High Dam.

As the United States Government saw the Czech arms deal, it was sure to touch off an uncontrolled arms race; American arms, it was thought, would not, even if they were given to Egypt, since they were legally tied to specific uses. Furthermore, the United States Government pointed out, it estimated that the likely terms upon which the arms were acquired would mortgage the Egyptian economy to the Soviet Union far into the future. These arguments failed to impress the Egyptian Government which pointed out both that it had tried unsuccessfully to acquire arms from the West and that it thought the Czech deal was a good trade. Syria and Saudi Arabia indicated their willingness to make similar arrangements. In the United States the fear grew that the "northern tier" had been hurdled.

Meanwhile border friction grew rather than lessened. Israeli forces attacked Syrian positions on October 22, Egyptian positions on November 2, and Syrian outposts on December 11. Clearly, this was an Israeli Governmental policy and to it the United States was opposed. When the U.N. Truce Supervision Organization (U.N.T.S.O.) called the Israeli action "a deliberate violation of the provisions of the general armistice agreement", the United States voted with the Security Council to condemn the Israeli acts. But in the Arab states there was no appreciation of Western attempts to be impartial. Egyptian anti-Western propaganda grew in bitterness and this propaganda played an important part in costing Great Britain her control over the Jordan army. In other Arab states, responsible political leaders privately expressed their fears that President Nasser had found his model not in Arabi Pasha but in Mehmet Ali Pasha—that his aim was not liberation of Egypt but regency over the Arabs. To the American public, Nasser began to assume the shape of a villain and the possible range of State Department actions in regard to him certainly narrowed.

Meanwhile, the Egyptian Government was anxious to secure the necessary dollar funds to construct the Aswan High Dam and had approached the International Bank for a loan. The Bank had agreed, contingent upon British and American participation to the amount of $70 million, to lend Egypt $200 million. In December, the United States had been prepared to agree to this, but Egypt did not at that time accept. When the president of the International Bank went to Cairo, the Egyptian Government "leaked" the rumour that agreement with the Soviet Union, on much better terms, was near. Retrospectively, this had been evaluated as an attempt to get the same reaction as the Czech arms deal, but this time the ploy did not work. The grant from the Soviet Union did not, at that time at least, materialize; then when President Nasser tried to reopen discussions with the United States, sending an ambassador to Washington to close the agreement, he met with a sharp and, in Egyptian eyes, humiliating rebuff. Secretary Dulles, having already met, but not countered, opposition to such a loan in the Congress, announced on July 20 that the United States could no longer consider participating. In its statement, moreover, the United States Government questioned "the ability of Egypt to devote adequate resources to assure the project's success" and also indicated its unfavourable view of the increasingly close ties between Egypt and the U.S.S.R. Infuriated by the "public insult", President Nasser struck out at the only available large target, the Suez Canal. In his Alexandria speech of July 26, he announced that the Universal Suez Maritime Canal Company had been nationalized.

At a Press Conference, on March 13, 1957, when asked about this sequence of moves, Secretary Dulles indicated that he did not regret the American refusal to aid in the Aswan Dam:

"No, I think if anything events have confirmed that [sic] fact that it would not have been a wise operation for us to have tried to conduct together. That was a gigantic proposition which involved expenditures of probably a billion and a half dollars, by far the largest operation of the kind ever known in the history of the world. It would have taken about 15 years of close association; it would have involved an austerity program on the part of Egypt which I think the people would have come to resent and would have blamed the foreigners who were the partners in the enterprise. The more we studied it the more we came to the conclusion that it was not a suitable project for the United States. . . ."

Asked further if he did not feel that the refusal of this aid had hastened the seizure of the Canal, Mr Dulles pointed out that subsequent information supplied by Tito indicated that plans had been drawn up two years prior to the crisis to seize the company, "and this may have provided the occasion, but if there had not been this occasion, I am quite sure another one would have been found".

With the benefit of hindsight, one might point out that Secretary Dulles was unquestionably right. Any nationalistic Egyptian Government was naturally going to look forward to the nationalization of the most significant "status symbol" in the country after the Suez military base, the Citadel, and Qasr al-Nil barracks, each of which had meant something quite different to the Egyptian than they did to the Westerner. Given this circumstance, it is now generally agreed in the United States that a more flexible position, with gradual withdrawal, might have preserved more—and certainly at far less damage to vital American and British interests—of the rights desired at Suez. Moreover, the circumstances of the withdrawal of the aid offer, which certainly the United States Government had the right to do, were such as to have forced any Egyptian leader, Nasser, Nagib, or Nahhas, to have acted to preserve national honour. It was, like Secretary Acheson's handling of the A.M.E.C. proposal, action with definite bad consequences but without probable benefits.

Reaction to nationalization of the Canal Company was swift. In brief, the foreign ministers of the United States, Great Britain, and France met in London and issued a statement on August 2. The first London Conference of the "User States" was held from August 16 to 23. It was there agreed that Mr Menzies should lead a five-man delegation to Cairo to present to President Nasser the proposals agreed to by 18 of the users. The Menzies delegation visited Cairo from September 3 to 9 but failed to reach any agreement. Up to this point, Western reaction had been so swift as to startle the Egyptian Government. The United States froze Egyptian funds in the United States, on the plea that it must be able to indemnify shippers who, while paying tolls to the Egyptian Government at Suez, might also be sued for tolls by the Canal Company in Europe. But already a fatal weakness appeared in the Western position. Greece refused to attend the conference and there was, within the conference, obvious disagreement as to the ways to negotiate a settlement and on the extent of pressure to be applied to Egypt. The attitude of Sir Anthony Eden was unmistakable but that of Mr Dulles was certainly unclear. The United States would not recommend to its citizens that they continue to serve in the canal, as other westerners resigned from their posts, but it also would not urge its shipping lines, all highly susceptible to Government pressure as the recipients of its subsidies, to boycott Suez. In these circumstances, President Nasser acted wisely, making every effort to keep the canal in operation so as to avoid charges of obstruction or incompetence, and waited for further disagreements to turn the *de facto* situation into one recognized as *de jure*.

On the eve of his departure for the Second London Conference, Secretary Dulles took what must have been read in Europe as a threatening tone:

"Let me make certain things quite clear; (1) The United States is dedicated to seeking by peaceful means [our rights] ... We are not, however, willing to accept for ourselves, nor do we seek from other nations, acceptance of an operating regime for the canal which falls short of recognizing the rights granted to canal users by the 1888 Convention ... we cannot be blind to the fact that conditions might become such that transit through the canal is impractical or greatly diminished. There must always be ways to assure the movement of vital supplies, particularly oil, to Western Europe...."

It was at this point that Mr Dulles unfolded his answer to the problem, the Canal Users Association, the precise nature of which was to become the major point of discussion at the Second London Conference. And at this conference, Mr Dulles issued a statement in which the main lines of American policy are clear—but clear, it must be admitted, in their exact emphasis, only in retrospect.

"Now we are faced here with a problem whereby great nations are faced with a great peril. It is a peril that they could readily remedy if they resorted to the methods which were lawful before this charter was adopted. Then, we wouldn't be sitting around here—perhaps somebody else wouldn't be sitting where he is, either. But those days, we hope, are past. There has been exercised, and is being exercised, a great restraint in the face of great peril. But you cannot expect that to go on indefinitely unless those of us who appreciate the problem, who are sympathetic with it, rally our forces to try to bring about a settlement in conformity with the principles of justice and international law."

On September 21, the United States subscribed to the "Co-operative Association of Suez Canal Users" which later was called the Suez Canal Users Association. Then five days later, the United States announced that it would back the United Kingdom and France in the forthcoming United Nations debate. In his press conference on that day, Secretary Dulles commented that ". . . the decision of the United States, at least, as I put it, [is] not to shoot its way through the canal. . . ." He went on to say that "there are pressures which gradually grow up, not artificially stimulated but as quite natural and inevitable. . . . But I do not believe that the situation is such now as to call for any drastic action like going to war." Boycott, he admitted, was no alternative, however, since "the idea that any grave economic blow can be struck at Egypt through the non-use of the canal is a quite false conception".

In the rush of events and in the circumstances, as we so far know of them, within the British Government and the French Government, these remarks did rather less than clarify exactly what the United States would agree to. As one of Mr Dulles's most able critics who shared basically the same approach to world politics, former Secretary Dean Acheson wrote, "It is fair to say that in the London conference, and in the episode of the Canal Users Association our conduct, whatever the intention may have been, led to expectations which proved false."[3] The position of the United States was, we can now say, throughout opposed to the use of force, but each statement, such as that of Secretary Dulles on October 6, was so worded as always to hedge with a "But those who are concerned about peace ought to be equally concerned about justice".

Indecision in the United States Government was certainly matched by confusing moves by the British Government; only the French and Israeli Governments appear, at the beginning of October, to have had clear plans. On October 10–11, when Israeli forces attacked Qalqilya,

[3] *Power and Diplomacy* (Harvard University Press, 1958), p. 112.

the British Government reaffirmed its treaty obligations to Jordan despite the fact that Jordan was obviously and rapidly moving in the direction of closer ties with Egypt. (On October 26, a unified military command of Jordan, Egypt, and Syria was established.) The British and French Governments certainly did not, however, keep the United States informed of what plans they had. Former Secretary Acheson, able to speak frankly but probably also able to draw on excellent sources of information, said bluntly that ". . . the British Government did not inform ours of its plans to use force. It is fair to go further and say that, at that stage, its conduct was deceitful."[4]

When reports of an Israeli mobilization reached President Eisenhower, he sent a personal message to Prime Minister Ben Gurion "expressing my grave concern and renewing a previous recommendation that no forcible initiative be taken which would endanger the peace". On October 28, the President again wrote to the Prime Minister. It is now known that already at that early date, the United States was applying strong pressure on Israel not to act. But the Israeli army invaded the next day; the following day came the Anglo-French ultimatum and on the 31st, the Anglo-French invasion. On the day of the ultimatum, the United States took the issue to the Security Council (where its resolution was vetoed by Britain and France) and on that same day, the President made a national radio and television address on the events in Hungary and the invasion of Egypt. In the course of his talk, Mr Eisenhower said:

"We believe these actions to have been taken in error. . . . The actions taken can scarcely be reconciled with the principles and purposes of the United Nations to which we have all subscribed. And beyond this, we are forced to doubt even if resort to war will for long serve the permanent interests of the attacking nations. . . . There can be no peace—without law. And there can be no law—if we were to invoke one code of international conduct for those who oppose us and another for our friends."

At the General Assembly, to which the United States had taken its vetoed resolution from the Security Council, Secretary Dulles on November 1 summed up, as perhaps no other statement he had ever made did more truly, the feelings of many Americans:

"I doubt that any delegates ever spoke from this forum with as heavy a heart as I have brought here tonight. We speak on a matter of vital importance, where the United States finds itself unable to agree with three nations with whom it has ties, deep friendship, admiration, and respect, and two of whom constitute our oldest, most trusted and reliable allies."

The General Assembly adopted 64-5, the United States resolution calling for an immediate ceasefire and withdrawal. But on November 3, this was rejected by France, Great Britain, and Israel. Negotiations were conducted by the U.N. Secretary General with Israel and Egypt, but both the United States and the Soviet Union took strong independent action. On November 4, the Soviet Government delivered a note to the British Government in which it "emphatically protests against these illegal actions by the United Kingdom and France and declares that the responsibility for all the possible consequences of those actions rests with the Governments of the United Kingdom and France". At the U.N., the United States supported a draft resolution introduced by Canada, Colombia, and Norway to establish a U.N. Command under General Burns of U.N.T.S.O., which was to organize the United Nations Emergency Force. On the same day, Soviet Foreign Minister Shepilov sent a note to the U.N. Security Council President declaring its readiness to send to Egypt "the air and naval forces necessary to defend Egypt and repulse the aggressors". Soviet Premier Bulganin wrote at the same time to President Eisenhower proposing "joint and immediate use" of the strong naval and air forces of the two powers to end the attack. In a statement from the White House, the United States immediately rejected the proposal saying that "neither Soviet nor any other military forces should now enter the Middle East area except under United Nations mandate. . . . The introduction of new forces under these circumstances would violate the United Nations Charter, and it would be the duty of all United Nations members, including the United States, to oppose any such effort." The U.S. note went on to contrast the Soviet attitude on Egypt with the Soviet intervention in Hungary. Similar Soviet notes were sent to Great Britain, France, and Israel in which the famous "threat" was issued:

> "In what position would Britain have found herself had she been attacked by more powerful states possessing all types of modern weapons of destruction? Indeed, such countries, instead of sending to the shores of Britain their naval or air forces, could have used other means, as, for instance, rocket equipment. . . . We are full of determination to crush the aggressor and reestablish peace in the East by using force.

"We hope that at this critical moment you will show due prudence and draw corresponding conclusions from this."

On October 7, Prime Minister Ben Gurion, far from indicating any fear of the Soviet attitude, which had included the withdrawing of the Soviet ambassador to Israel, spoke of the "glorious military operation . . . an unprecedented feat in Jewish history and . . . rare in the world's history". But on the same day, the General Assembly once again called upon Israel to withdraw, and President Eisenhower again wrote to express his "deep concern" at the refusal of the Israeli Government to withdraw its army from Egyptian territory. In reply, the following day, in the face of strong American pressure the Prime Minister agreed to comply but indicated that the problem of the Sinai hostilities could not be separated from the context of the whole aftermath of the Palestine war. As Israel saw the steps toward peace, they must include, along with evacuation of Sinai, the end of the economic boycott of Israel, direct negotiations between Israel and the Arab states, and freedom of passage for Israeli ships through the Straits of Tiran and through Suez.

Israeli demands were regarded with sympathy in Washington since it was the opinion of the United States Government that Egypt had done much to provoke the attack on the one hand, and on the other that a return to the *status quo ante* was dangerous. Yet, the United States Government also was worried about the implications of a solution brought about by the use of force, for if the invasion could be reckoned, even indirectly, a success then the dangers of *coups de main* were certainly increased. Consequently, both in public and in private, the American Government assured Israel that it would do all in its power to settle the outstanding problems of the *status quo ante* but that, as Ambassador Lodge said in the General Assembly on several occasions and Secretary Dulles affirmed in dispatches to the Israeli Government, the United States agreed with the Secretary General that "withdrawal is a preliminary and essential phase in a development through which a stable basis may be laid for peaceful conditions in the area".

With the British and French position, the United States Government felt, possibly, less sympathy in that the actions of such close allies—particularly in the context of N.A.T.O.—put the United States Government in a position of acute embarrassment. It was felt also that the Anglo-French invasion had at least mitigated the effects of the brutal Soviet repression of Hungary and was thus not only irresponsible but tragic. Considerable relief was felt in Washington when the last of the Anglo-French force was evacuated on December 23, and U.N.E.F. forces began their forward movement into Sinai.

The negotiations leading to the final Israeli agreement to withdraw unconditionally on March 1 need not detain us as the position of the United States Government was consistent—unconditional withdrawal prior to any discussion of the inadequacies of the *status quo ante*.

It was at this point that the United States had to try to pick up the tangled lines of its various alliances and to reassess the general context of its non-Soviet foreign policy. Here, in the opinion of this writer, the United States ceased to show the leadership and courage which had led it "with a heavy heart" to stand by its principles in the dangerous days of November. But, before discussing the development of the Eisenhower Doctrine, one may venture certain observations on the Suez crisis.

The following facts seem quite clear: (1) the United States was throughout the crisis opposed to the use of force. However, in the attempt to apply pressure to Egypt, to bring about a compromise, Secretary Dulles was prepared to hedge about the possibility of a final resort to force. This did not bring about the desired results in Egypt but may have convinced the British, French, and Israeli Governments that the United States would not strongly oppose their action. (2) The United States must accept a large measure of tactical responsibility for the nationalization of the Suez Canal. The manner of the refusal, after long negotiations and prior agreement, of aid to Egypt was an action which demanded and got a counter action. (3) Both the British and American Governments, at their highest levels, failed to comprehend or at least properly to weigh the psychological importance of a legacy of inferiority and humiliation which for Egyptians was symbolized by foreign control of Suez. Some analysis of these motivations and a timely concession on such issues as sovereignty over Suez might have forestalled the entire problem. (4) If the Suez crisis did not make the brutal repression in Hungary possible, it at least neutralized the strong effects that repression would otherwise have had on world opinion. The Indian position was squarely in line with that of most of Asia and Africa. (5) If the United States was to attempt to hold together a broad and at times mutually hostile coalition of Europe and Asia, it must have firm, clear, and definite policy assumptions and goals by which crises could be controlled. In the Eisenhower Doctrine, it attempted to accomplish this purpose.

A part of the justification for the British intervention in Suez was given in the Commons on December 3 by Foreign Secretary Lloyd as

"Soviet mischief making". "The large supply of Soviet arms to Colonel Nasser," said Mr Lloyd, "put him very much under Soviet influence. The Baghdad Pact gave a measure of security against direct Soviet penetration from the North, but the arming of Syria and Egypt, was no doubt intended to turn its flank also." It was this element which rapidly re-emerged from momentary eclipse in American thought just as soon as the local crisis had become manageable. On January 5, at a time in which the United States was attempting at the United Nations and through direct pressure to bring about a withdrawal of Israeli forces in Egypt, President Eisenhower turned his attention back to the threat of the Soviet Union in the Middle East. In the course of his address to Congress, the President said:

"All this instability [in the Middle East] has been heightened and, at times, manipulated by International Communism. . . . Russia's interest in the Middle East is solely that of power politics. Considering her announced purpose of Communizing the world, it is easy to understand her hope of dominating the Middle East. . . . [If this came about] Western Europe would be endangered just as though there had been no Marshall Plan, no North Atlantic Treaty Organization. The free nations of Asia and Africa, too, would be placed in serious jeopardy."

The U.N., said President Eisenhower, had shown its abilities when faced by nations with a decent respect for the opinions of mankind, but in Hungary the situation was otherwise. Therefore,

". . . a greater responsibility now develops upon the United States. We have shown, so that none can doubt, our dedication to the principle that force shall not be used internationally for any aggressive purpose and that the integrity and independence of the nations of the Middle East should be inviolate. Seldom in history has a nation's dedication to principle been tested as severely as ours during recent weeks."

The President went on to propose a joint Congressional-Presidential declaration embodying three features: (1) Provision for the United States to co-operate with nations in the area to build up their economic strength. To this end $200 million yearly for the discretionary use of the President was requested. (2) Greater flexibility for the President to use funds already allocated to assist any nation or group of nations desiring military assistance and co-operation; and (3) Permission to use the "armed forces of the United States to secure and protect the territorial integrity and political independence of such nations, requesting such aid, against overt armed aggression from any nation controlled by International Communism".

In testimony before the Congress, Secretary Dulles pointed out that the Eisenhower Doctrine was a continuation of a policy begun years before; the developmental steps he traced were the 1947 Truman Doctrine, 1948 Marshall Plan, 1949 N.A.T.O., 1950 American action in Korea, 1954 Caracas Declaration on Communism in the Western Hemisphere and the South-east Asia Collective Defence Treaty, 1955 American defence of Taiwan and Penghu.

". . . though the needs have been different, and the Constitutional methods have been different, there have been basic underlying similarities. . . . In each case we proceeded from the premise that, as it was put by President Truman in his Greek-Turkey message, 'totalitarian regimes imposed upon free peoples, by direct or in-direct aggression, undermine the foundations of international peace and hence the security of the United States'."

The Eisenhower Doctrine was neither a new policy nor a Middle Eastern policy. It was aimed, as it were, at two targets: it was meant to warn the Soviet Union that under no circumstances, even such as had arisen in the Suez crisis, would the United States permit the forcible entry of the Soviet Union into the Middle East. Its second target was domestic in that it attempted to galvanize public and Congressional opinion behind both current and future aid programmes and other measures in a way which would give the administration greater flexibility. In making these appear as essential to the security of the United States and in linking American policy in the Middle East to the threat of Communism, the United States Government tried to lift the complex issues confronting it in the Middle East above the level of ordinary Middle Eastern policies, which are subject to strong domestic political pressures, and to make of them a national programme, a pro-gramme which the administration tried, unsuccessfully, to name the "American Doctrine". In this way, it seems to the present writer, one can understand the curious timing and the curious lack of Middle Eastern content. But to accomplish the domestic American aims and to re-emphasize a well-known position, the Government may have paid a heavy price in the Middle East and Asia. It seemed to many in Asia that the Eisenhower Doctrine had no relevance to the current scene. At a time when impressive evidence had just been given of the dangers of Western aggression, with the Tripartite Declaration broken by two

of its three signers and with Israel still in occupation of Egyptian territory, the United States was warning of the dangers of the Soviet
Union, a power which had offered, however insincerely, to "crush the
aggressors". Events in Hungary, however clearly these may have
seemed to spell the real danger, were obfuscated in the Asian mind by
the resurgent ghost of Western imperialism. In short, the Eisenhower
Docrine did not address itself to what many in Asia and Africa thought
to be the "clear and present danger".

Congress passed the Eisenhower Doctrine as a joint resolution on
March 9, 1957, and on the same day the President appointed Mr James
P. Richards, former chairman of the House Foreign Affairs Committee,
as his special assistant to investigate the Middle Eastern scene relative
to the new doctrine. The next step was to round up support for the
new doctrine; it was essentially on this mission that Mr Richards set
off to the Middle East. Like the doctrine itself, his mission was largely
redundant since all that he gained was the public endorsement of the
doctrine by those states which had already indicated their friendly
attitude toward the same policy in a former guise. But upon his return,
Ambassador Richards spoke glowingly on June 13 to the House
Foreign Affairs Committee of his mission. "This new departure, this
entirely American line of action, evoked a heart-warming trust from
the nations of the area." On his trip, Mr Richards said, he had man-
aged to give out $120 million of which one-half went for economic aid.
And his optimism was echoed by other officials. Assistant Secretary
Rountree, on May 16, affirmed that American policies were "definitely" achieving their goals. "International Communism", reads the
first report of the Richards' mission on August 5, 1957, "has been
put on notice . . . and the nations of the area are encouraged to help
themselves. . . ."

That the United States had not found the answer to the instability
of the area some had expected, however, was becoming apparent.
The Jordan crisis of the spring had been a jolt but the "Syrian crisis" of
August and September was a clear test. On August 6, the Soviet
Government agreed to provide large amounts of economic aid to
Syria; on August 15, the Syrian Chief of Staff was replaced by a man
regarded in Washington as pro-Soviet. Rumours of American unhap-
piness with these moves reached such a point that officials of the United
States Embassy in Damascus were expelled and, in retaliation, the
Syrian ambassador was asked to leave Washington. On August 22,
U.S. Ambassador Loy Henderson, who was best known in the Middle
East for the role he was thought to have played in the counter *coup*

d'état which unseated Mossadeq, was sent on a flying trip to the areas surrounding Syria. Sixth Fleet manœuvres were held just off the Syrian coast. On September 7, Secretary Dulles said that:

> "At a meeting of Mr Henderson, Mr Rountree and myself with President Eisenhower, Mr Henderson ... reported that he had found in the Near East deep concern at the apparently growing Soviet Communist domination of Syria and the large build-up there of Soviet bloc arms."

Arms shipments were announced to Jordan (by airlift) and to Lebanon, Iraq, and Saudi Arabia.

These moves were followed by a statement from Secretary Dulles that "Turkey now faces growing military danger from the major build-up of arms in Syria". Nowhere in the Middle East was this taken at face value. Given the facts—the Syrian army contained only about 50,000 men, mostly lacking in battle experience, whose presence on the Israeli frontier was necessary, whose equipment was new and for which they were poorly trained versus the Turkish army of half a million men (the largest field force in N.A.T.O.) who had been armed and trained for a decade by the United States, and, in being able to rely upon N.A.T.O. guarantees, were able to deploy on the Syrian frontier —it is not surprising that many in the Middle East thought that the United States was looking for an excuse to employ the Eisenhower Doctrine. When the Soviet Government protested, and when no coup materialized—none perhaps having ever been planned—the Soviet Union got the credit while the United States suffered, even in the minds of those who had wanted a change in the Syrian Government, a signal defeat.

It is now clear that the United States was not prepared to take decisive action to block the Soviet Union's offer of aid, but in giving the impression that it intended to do so both had to back down and to be damned for having opposed the good that might result from such aid. The fact was that simple opposition to the Soviet Union was not sufficient policy to guide in the Middle East. It might well be that had the United States been prepared to encourage the Syrian Government to accept aid—which it could not in any case prevent—and to offer itself to assist in supervising and controlling such aid, to make it conform to Syrian wishes, that not only would the United States have suffered no defeat but might have gained considerable credit. As it was, the actions of the United States Government were both futile and damaging to its position. But if the Syrian crisis of the fall showed the shortfalls of the Eisenhower Doctrine, the Lebanese crisis of the spring and summer showed its dangers.

On May 8, 1958, the editor of the Beirut newspaper *at-Talaghraf* was shot and this act touched off an already tense and smouldering atmosphere. The contributing causes of the tension were many but one element of import here was the excessive, in the eyes of many Lebanese, identification of the Government of Lebanon with United States policy particularly in so far as this was opposed to President Nasser of Egypt. The Richards Mission had been interpreted in the Middle East as a demand that the Middle Eastern states leave the neutralist position which many had found attractive and "stand up to be counted", a posture for which the United States was prepared to pay cash. Thus, on May 10 the United States Information Service (U.S.I.S.) library in Tripoli was sacked; on the 12th Beirut was blockaded; on the 14th the United States said it was doubling the marine force with the Sixth Fleet; on the 16th announced that it would shortly send tanks to Lebanon; and on the 17th stated that it was considering sending troops to Lebanon if requested. On the 18th the U.S.S.R. accused the United States of interfering in Lebanese domestic affairs. Great Britain and the United States agreed to joint action if needed and on the 25th the R.A.F. delivered arms to Lebanon. By June 3 the last (the fifth) U.S.I.S. Centre was closed.

Lebanon had become, meanwhile, a sort of rope in the tug of war between President Nasser and Secretary Dulles. The United States maintained its offer to send troops if required but was constantly worried by the use made of the arms it had supplied for regular military units—these were often given over to partisan forces. On July 3, the United Nations observer group reported "no evidence" of mass infiltration as charged by the Lebanese Government. On July 15, however, some 5,000 United States Marines landed near Beirut airport.

The precipitating cause, of course, had nothing to do with Lebanon directly but was the *coup d'état* in Baghdad on July 14. Like the Lebanese civil war, the coup in Baghdad was the result of many factors, but of these two crucial ones were: (1) The identification of the Iraqi Government with the United States Government to such an extent, in the opinion of a large section of the Iraqi population, that the Iraq Government was not acting on Iraqi or Arab interests but on behalf of the British and American Governments. (2) It seems likely that the attempt to use Iraqi troops to stabilize the Middle Eastern situation may have been the event which touched off the coup. In short, it may be that the very act of getting the Governments in the Middle East to "stand up and be counted" forced them into a weaker domestic position and so produced results opposite to those expected in Washington. Events have shown, moreover, that the Baghdad Pact was a fair weather pact, strong on paper but fatally weak at the centre in a crisis, and had also raised the question of the utility of such pacts when the aims they included were not popular in the member states.

The *coup d'état* in Baghdad clearly caught the United States as much by surprise as it did the senior officials of the Iraq Government. Yet, there had been ample warnings from observers both in the United States and in England. The fact that these warnings were not heeded gives rise to the question as to whether or not the assumptions made in the Eisenhower Doctrine could comprehend such warnings. In any event, the United States was clearly left with no reasonable move. It could not seriously maintain that the coup in Iraq was due to Communist subversion, for the Communists had almost no part in it. Moreover, having landed a large force in Lebanon with more troops and material in the "pipe line" to Lebanon and having compromised the Lebanese Government by that landing, the United States was faced with a most delicate series of decisions. It is fortunate that the Lebanese gift for compromise quickly showed itself in the agreement of General Fuad Shihab to become president; so that the United States was able gracefully, to the tune of heavy spending in the Beirut markets, to withdraw its troops from Lebanon.

No answer had been found to the new situation in Iraq and indeed it is possible that no meaningful action—and perhaps as crucial—no meaningful inaction within the framework of the Eisenhower Doctrine was possible. Baghdad, from being the centre post of the Baghdad Pact, became one of the most anti-American cities in the Middle East, and the United States, without adequate policy guides, had been forced passively to watch the new government make firmer and closer alliances with the Soviet bloc.

Reacting from the situation produced by events in Iraq, the United States apparently has drifted back into closer ties with President Nasser of the United Arab Republic; President Nasser, reacting from the same events, has himself turned sharply against the Soviet Union. It is thus that the new powers in the Middle East, the United States and the Soviet Union, find their best laid schemes gang aft a-gley, with a partly pro-Western U.A.R. armed with Russian tanks facing in growing hostility a partly pro-Soviet Iraq armed with Anglo-American equipment.

With an obvious relish for irony, James F. Byrnes once ascribed the origins of the Truman Doctrine to Marx's advice that "if the other powers hold firm, Russia is sure to retire in a very decent manner". Ironic it is that the "containment" aspect of American policy should be considered as a legacy of Marx for surely much more might be ascribed to him in the second facet of American policy, economic assistance. It has been shown above that the United States came to a position in which its assumptions on the power of economics to control the minds of men differed little from those of the Soviet Union. This is not to say that such an assumption was ever so consciously or explicitly set forth as it has been in Soviet foreign policy analysis but the assumption has, through a force of circumstance, simply and naturally been accepted by many who would be shocked by its philosophical implications. Given the past political assumptions of the United States, this fact requires some explanation.

In the first place, it should be noted that isolationism was not dead in the United States at the end of World War II. However, its main lines had been sapped. Given the recognition by responsible Americans on the one hand that the actuality of their power required American participation in world affairs and on the other the general mood of the public, which was in 1947 weary of war but also unrequited by war, stirred far more than in World War I to action and consequently more than at the end of World War I restless in its return to peace, the United States was ready to accept commitments which fell short of requiring a return to military duty but which would both stir the heart and stimulate industry.

In the second place, the forces of isolationism were redirected. Whereas at the end of World War I, a strong factor in the withdrawal of the United States was disillusionment with the wickedness of the nearer allies, at the end of World War II, this was muted by the early withdrawal, in part, of those allies themselves. Neither could wartime hatred of Germany be sustained, even by the horror of the extermination camp exhibits, toward a seemingly destroyed foe. Rather, what had been disillusionment with the rest of the world in 1920 became in 1946-7 fear and suspicion concentrated upon the Soviet Union. Events in Eastern Europe, Iran, Greece, Turkey, and elsewhere immediately contributed to this and these emotions were multiplied by the Chinese revolution and the Korean war. Within the United States, fear of the Soviet Union found a natural expression in many of those individuals and groups who would, perhaps, in other times have been isolationists. So that domestic political forces were galvanized behind international programmes which were opposed to "atheistic communism".

In the third place, given the identification of the Soviet Union *cum* Communism as *the* enemy, other problems paled into insignificance. Attention to other fears and hatreds could detract from the determination to fight the central foe and so were disruptive or worse. President Truman sounded this note in requesting Congressional support for his doctrine. Through the Eisenhower Doctrine, it was the central theme of American foreign policy thought. For this reason such issues as the political philosophies of America's allies or the mutual incompatibility of their aspirations had to be suppressed or at least kept *sotto voce*. In no case, even in the Suez crisis, could they be allowed for long to divert attention from the real and ever-present menace of the Soviet Union. Hence, it was often inconvenient to place stress on the domestic political beliefs of Americans or upon the sort of political arrangements they would desire for allies: these expressions of political intent might diminish the force of the grand alliance which alone could contain the Soviet Union. Given this assumption, it was reasonable that little attempt would be made to measure the political worth, in American terms, of allies; the "Free World" came to include the widest range of political structures known to man.

As a corollary of this, some attempt had to be made to find out what it was that attracted men to Communism. Poverty was the immediate answer. In this problem, the United States had some experience and had, in the New Deal and in subsequent programmes, evolved solutions which by reallocation of resources between the several states and between social classes, "primed the pumps" of national wealth. It seemed obvious that some such effort was needed overseas. Consequently, in the Truman Doctrine, the Marshall Plan, Point IV, the Mutual Security Act, and the Eisenhower Doctrine, economic assistance played a major role. It was assumed, for example, in the attempt to get Jordan and Israel to work together to develop the Jordan River that economic assistance could lessen regional hostility and hence allow for a reallocation of energies against the real foe, the Soviet Union, and that economic programmes could both end the dissatisfactions which give rise to Communism and could win for co-operating Middle Eastern governments sufficient loyalty from their citizens that they could co-operate with the United States in its major aim. These assumptions were rarely challenged[5] until after the Iraq *coup d'état*. In Iraq, it was discovered that many, who were basically opposed to Communism themselves, felt strongly that their ills were due to other factors, that economic development—within their current political context—was not the answer to their yearnings—which were often psychological and often arose from political desires—and, even more importantly, that economic measures could not be evaluated, as the United States had attempted to do, on the static scale of a dismal past but rather were constantly evaluated on the dynamic rise in expectations which grow out of the realization that change is possible—and being possible is also possible dramatically, radically, and immediately. Baghdad left the United States with more than a void in the centre of the Pact; it left the serious doubt whether the assumptions of American policy were sufficient as bases for a Middle Eastern policy.

In conclusion, it can be said that American policy has started from the whole and has merely accommodated the parts; that while this sort of approach to policy has advantages in consistency it lacks in scope. The Baghdad coup showed that it would have been useful to have begun long ago to analyse in detail the complex pieces of politics which in some sort of ill-shapen way must make a policy not only for the Soviet Union but also for the Middle East.

[5] A notable exception is Z. Brzezinski, "The Politics of Underdevelopment" in *Journal of World Politics*, October 1956.

© WILLIAM R. POLK 1961

"DRAGOMANIA": THE DRAGOMANS OF THE BRITISH EMBASSY IN TURKEY

By Allan Cunningham

THE LEVANTINE DRAGOMANS, or interpreters, who served the British embassy in Constantinople during the major part of the nineteenth century, were discussed and described in terms of opprobrium by so many people—travellers, ambassadors, Foreign Office clerks, historians—that their name became synonymous with unreliability, inefficiency, and disloyalty. David Urquhart called this sentiment of hostility "dragomania" and we can put it in one kind of perspective by assigning it tentative dates. It may have received its original stimulus from the young and hypercritical Stratford Canning during his first (1810–12) embassy to the Porte; it certainly gathered force with his second and third missions to Turkey. A further impulse came with the advent of Palmerston as Foreign Secretary in 1830. Plans for reform were discussed, rather perfunctorily considering the outcry against the dragomans, from then until 1840, and a project for the introduction of Englishmen into the interpreter service was actually put in hand in 1841. One might well enquire why a function as indispensable to the tasks of the Turkey embassy as that of interpreter was left for so long in such supposedly unsatisfactory hands.

The word dragoman, from the Turkish *tercüman*, is normally translated "interpreter", but if the functions of the dragomans employed by the European embassies had not traditionally involved much more than attendance at interviews and the translation of diplomatic and commercial documents they would not have become the controversial figures they were. In the great majority of cases eighteenth and nineteenth-century dragomans were Levantines, that is, the children of European, but not necessarily purely European, families long resident in the East. Whether Italian, Greek, Austrian, Russian, Vlach or British, such men ordinarily lived in the same district of Constantinople, usually in the "Frank quarter" of Pera or, more rarely, the Greek *Fener*. Only in the nineteenth century did a sharpening appreciation of the

importance of embassy security lead the Foreign Office to examine
these domestic arrangements.

From the beginnings of the British embassy in the days of the first
Elizabeth, families of Italian extraction predominated in its interpreter
service, and the name of Pisani runs like a thread through over two
centuries of Levant Company and Foreign Office archives. The
prominence of such families explains the percolation of words like
bagnio and *seraglio* into common use among embassy officials and in
the pages of the correspondence. These families, strange and rather
tragic wanderers between two worlds, the one in which they lived
and the other they served, knew the tongues of both. Probably any
Pisani, generation after generation, could think in Greek, Turkish, and
Italian, the languages most heard in the streets and on the wharves of
the Golden Horn. Italian and Greek were common in the world of
trade and commerce. Turkish itself and, of the European tongues,
French were the means of diplomatic exchange. As to intercourse
between ambassadors and dragomans, the British ministers were
insisting on a competence in English, though still accepting men
with a greater skill in French, by the third quarter of the eighteenth
century.

Besides acting as intermediaries at interviews and translating the
correspondence exchanged between the embassies and the Turkish
government, dragomans were negotiators in their own right, and frequently very skilled ones too. Marriages between Levantine and Turkish
families were rare, even perilous, but close friendships were common
enough and in this way dragomans often came to be on amicable
terms with high officials or ministers in the Ottoman bureaucracy.
They could be expected to know a good deal about Ottoman institutions, politics, and diplomatic etiquette; what was of more obvious and
immediate usefulness, they generally had means of knowing the balance
of power in the *Divan* at any given moment, the policies and opinions
currently predominant there, and the men who stood highest in the
Sultan's favour. In general terms, it might be said that the poorer type
of dragoman in any embassy was a mere scavenger of gossip, whereas
the best of them were valued and trusted servants. There is no shortage
of tributes paid by British ministers to these versatile and nimble-
witted men, in either the eighteenth or nineteenth centuries. Sutton,
who stands at the threshold of the eighteenth, treated his "Drugger-
man" as friend as well as agent, and this was the usual relationship.
This particular dragoman enjoyed confidential communication with
the office of the |*Reis Efendi* (Head of the Turkish Chancery) and

the Grand Vezir's *kâhya* (deputy), and obtained military intelligence regarding the 1711 campaign on the Pruth against the Russians from the Sultan's head chamberlain and other "persons who certainly enter very far into the secrets of this government".[1] In 1749 the services of the Pisani who was then dragoman to Sir James Porter were thought sufficiently meritorious for George II to confer on him the rather grand title of "His Majesty's Translator of the Oriental Languages".[2] This Pisani's son, Bartholomew, was the friend and confidant of a series of ambassadors including Ainslie (1780–94), Elgin (1799–1802), and Liston (1812–20).

Until the late eighteenth century, the incumbent of the British embassy on the Bosphorus was regarded by the Turks, quite reasonably, as the representative of his King before all else, but in reality the ambassador was the salaried servant of the Levant Company, which entrusted him with the supervision of British mercantile interests in the realm of the Grand Signior. In the course of time, British governments had come to show growing interest in the appointment until, by the eighteenth century, the Company was simply ratifying the government's choice of candidate, while still paying his salary. Successive governments made contributions in various forms to the upkeep of the Turkey embassy, but it was not until 1804 that the ambassador severed most of his connexions with the Levant Company. Up to 1804 he remained at the mercy of two sets of instructions, a position which became increasingly intolerable once the Foreign Office, itself newly established in 1782, found it necessary to watch the encroachment of Russia on Turkey with greater concern than heretofore. The dramatic lessons in Near Eastern strategy and diplomacy administered by Napoleon finally made it imperative for the government to assume complete control of the embassy. Charles Arbuthnot, appointed British minister in 1804, was told to give his whole attention to political matters, and the Company was advised to find itself a consul-general to supervise its commercial interests.[3]

As the position of ambassador had been anomalous for over a century, it is not surprising that the status and loyalties of the dragomans remained unresolved for some years more. Even after 1804, they

---

[1] Akdes Nimet Kurat (ed.), *The Despatches of Sir Robert Sutton* (London, 1957), Introduction, p. 9.

[2] Duke of Bedford to Porter, 12 October 1749, enclo. in Liston to Mr Cooke, Private, 18 September 1812, F.O. 78/79; A. C. Wood, "The English Embassy in Constantinople", *Eng. Hist. Review*, xl (1925), 538.

[3] A. C. Wood, *History of the Levant Company* (London, 1935), p. 184.

were still appointed and paid by the Company although ambassadors were making growing demands upon the services of at least one of them, and at times of political stress sometimes employing two out of the four available. The pressure of diplomatic business on the embassy went on increasing as the official correspondence reveals; Ainslie's mainly commercial correspondence for a dozen pre-revolutionary years was smaller in amount than Elgin's political despatches for the urgent years of 1800–2. Simultaneously, the dragomans found their work altering in character as well as amount, and the ambassadors could spare the dragomans correspondingly less for the work of the Company. This produced friction between the embassy and the British merchants in Pera, who saw the embassy staff from the minister downwards as their paid servants. The dispute reached an acute stage as early as Elgin's embassy.

Lord Elgin, who went out as ambassador in 1799, found four dragomans and four *giovani di lingua*, or student interpreters, in the service of the Levant Company.[4] Anthony Dané, the first dragoman, was very old and soon retired, the first *giovane*, George Calavro, moving up to fourth dragoman. The man Elgin took as his political dragoman was, almost inevitably, Bartholomew Pisani, second dragoman before Dané retired, and a person of unequalled political experience and linguistic talent. Pisani had thirty years' Company service behind him, had acted as embassy treasurer, embassy secretary, even *chargé d'affaires*, and was also permanent *cancellier*, or archivist, to the Company. Elgin's wish to make the most of Pisani's diplomatic experience in his dealings with senior Turks precipitated a long and acrimonious quarrel with Spencer Smith, the Company's local agent. Smith had been appointed *locum tenens* by the Foreign Office until Elgin should arrive from England, and was piqued when it became necessary to surrender the ministerial title. Rediscovering an intense loyalty to the Company, he organized the British merchants to protest to the Foreign Office against Elgin's annexation of Pisani although, in the first instance, Smith himself had suggested it. Elgin, on his side, repeatedly told the Foreign Secretary that diplomatic work must have precedence over Company interests, for a dragoman as for the ambassador. The casual, trading days were gone; the contest with the French Directory had now spread to the East, and the challenge needed to be met with every possible resource. Grenville, President of the Levant Company as well as Foreign Secre-

---

[4] The dragomans were Anthony Dané, Bartholomew Pisani, Antonio Pisani, Francis Chabert; the *giovani* were George Calavro, Frederick Pisani, Felix Navon, Constantin Aidé.

tary, was ideally placed to solve the issue, and did so by recalling Smith, leaving the disposal of the dragomans, and the supervision of the Company's interests, solely in the hands of Elgin.

Elgin was a kindly and considerate man, and with his accession to uncontested power he undertook the task, long overdue, of putting the dragomans' salaries on a more definite basis. In recent years, inflationary tendencies had depressed the value of the Turkish piastre. This created financial difficulties for recipients of fixed piastre salaries, such as the ambassador himself and the consuls in the Levant, but the dragomans were the worst off because their income had been dwindling with the diminishing sale of embassy protections. These protections secured for a purchaser immunity from the Ottoman legal process and the enjoy-ment of British extra-territorial rights under the Capitulations, and were thus very attractive to Christian and Jewish merchants, refugees from Ottoman justice, and the like. Dragomans traditionally drew a commission from petitioners whose claims for protection were success-fully introduced to the ambassador, and large sums were made in this way until Sultan Selim III's ministers felt constrained to protest against the excessive number of Ottoman subjects sheltering under the Capitu-lations. The European embassies were in no position to resist the pres-sure the Turks put upon them to curtail the practice, and the British dragomans' interest in a fixed salary seems to date from the early 'nineties, when their commission from the sale of protections was shrinking from year to year. Elgin succeeded in introducing fixed and graded salaries, with no fees attaching to them, but they were far from generous and made no allowance for the upward spiral of commodity prices in Constantinople after 1794. To the end of his embassy, Elgin kept the financial predicament of his dragomans before Grenville's attention, though without further tangible result.[5]

In January 1807, the Russian and British ministers severed relations with the Turkish Government in protest against the ascendancy of the French minister, Sebastiani, in the councils of the Porte. They both withdrew on British warships. The dragomans, as local residents, and British-protected persons rather than British subjects, naturally stayed

[5] Copies of Bartholomew Pisani to Liston (undated); Elgin to Pisani, 3 January 1803, in Liston to Cooke, Private, 18 September 1812, F.O. 78/79; Adair to Canning, Separate, 24 September 1809, F.O. 78/64. The practice of selling *berats* or patents of protection to Jewish and Armenian merchants to enable them to avoid Ottoman taxation was not stopped finally until the signing of the Treaty of the Dardanelles, 1809. Liston believed some English ambassadors had made as much as £2-3,000 per annum from selling *berats*; see Liston to Grenville, 25 April 1795, F.O. 78/16.

behind, and were in real danger when Admiral Duckworth appeared soon afterwards with warships and hostile intentions. They kept indoors while the Turkish capital feverishly organized its defences, but Bartholomew Pisani was seized and imprisoned for two years, to be liberated in 1808, when Adair came to repair relations. Pisani was sent down to the Dardanelles, where the treaty of 5 January 1809 was ultimately signed, and it was his command of languages and insight into the Turkish mind, as revealed on this occasion, which gave Adair the high regard for the dragomans which he never lost. On reaching the Porte, Adair paid out 11,000 piastres to save the dragomans from "immediate indigence", and asked the Foreign Office to treat the sum as a gift rather than arrears of salary. He also forwarded a petition from all his "Drogmans and Jeunes de langues" urgently requesting an adjustment of their salaries.[6]

Lacking an official residence, Adair passed his eastern sojourn in a house rented from his political dragoman, Bartholomew Pisani, who was his most-used intermediary with the Turks during 1809.[7] By 1810 Pisani was ailing and it was necessary to bring Francis Chabert, nominally the third dragoman, into the diplomatic work. Chabert was a very brilliant linguist, with the additional distinction that, during the fire which swept Pera in 1810, he attended at the endangered embassy while his own house burned to the ground.[8] Thus Adair began the habit, followed by all his successors, of choosing his political dragoman without regard for the Levant Company's order of seniority. There was no interference with the Company's salary gradation, the "political" interpreter simply receiving an extra £400 responsibility pay. Adair's confidant was the third dragoman; Ponsonby employed both the third and fourth as his. Generally speaking, Adair treated all his staff with consideration, supported their petitions to the Foreign Office zealously, and entertained them under his rented roof in the traditional eighteenth-

---

[6] Adair to Canning, 18 November 1808, F.O. 78/60; 1,6 January 1809, F.O. 78/63; 5 January 1810, F.O. 78/68. The dragomans' petition is in the despatch of 6 January 1809. The exchange rate in 1809 was 18 piastres to the £; it was 12½ in 1792.

[7] The derelict state of the embassy building, and the consequences of several visitations by Turkish officials "pour faire l'inventoire des Meubles" after Arbuthnot's withdrawal, are described in Adair to Canning, 15 September 1809, F.O. 78/64; repair work is discussed in Adair to Canning, 5 January 1810, F.O. 78/68.

[8] Adair to Wellesley, 22 April 1810, F.O. 78/68; Stratford Canning to Wellesley, 16 May 1810, F.O. 78/70; Lane-Poole, Life of Stratford Canning (London, 1888), i, 83.

century way. All his dragomans had access to the archives, and Chabert was taken completely into his confidence. Yet ironically, Adair had as his secretary a young man who was to change all this by keeping the staff at arm's length, distrusting dragomans as a point of principle, and seeking neither their friendship nor trust. This was Stratford Canning, who was only 23 when he succeeded Adair as head of the mission in 1810.

Stratford's dislikes were comprehensive, and included the East ("A few months have passed away—my curiosity is satisfied—the novelty is gone"), the diplomatic career, the Turks, the salary, the European community and the dragomans.[9] Lane-Poole says it was Stratford who first envisaged the possibility of a "regular school of student-interpreters composed of English gentlemen" and that "he used every effort to improve the tone of the Dragomans and raise them above suspicion". But in a despatch which Castlereagh sent to Stratford's successor, Robert Liston, the Foreign Secretary explains that one Terrick Hamilton will be coming out from England as "chief interpreter" when "duly qualified", and this "new Institution", Castlereagh adds, was the arrangement of his predecessor, Wellesley.[10] Since Adair came home while Wellesley was still at the Foreign Office and Stratford did not, and as Stratford had no private correspondence with Wellesley, it seems likely that the "new Institution" was inspired by Adair. Adair was irritated, as Elgin had been, by the demands made upon his time by the British merchants in Pera, and disliked the divided loyalties the dragomans necessarily felt. His allocation of the purely Company work to Antonio Pisani and Calavro, and the employment of Bartholomew Pisani and Chabert for all political negotiations, was his own attempt to resolve the problem. Wellesley's intention to supply the ambassador with a Turkish-speaking lieutenant without disturbing the existing hierarchy of local dragomans, fits in with Adair's probable recommendations rather than with the known sentiments of Stratford.[11] However, the latter's dislike of the dragomans, from the start of his Eastern career, is insisted upon by his biographer, and was more than likely from what is known of his mistrustful, misanthropic character.[12] Where Adair spoke of "the ancient and honourable" family of Pisani, Stratford called the interpreters "mongrels". When he came home in

---

[9] See in particular Stratford's letters to Richard Wellesley, 9 November 1809 and to his cousin George Canning, 8 January 1810, in Lane-Poole, *op. cit.*, i, 70, 77.

[10] Lane-Poole, *op. cit.*, i, 136, n.; Castlereagh to Liston, 27 March, Liston to Castlereagh, 11 July, 13 December 1812, F.O. 78/79.

[11] Adair to Canning, 9 April 1809, with two enclosures, F.O. 78/63.

[12] Lane-Poole, *op. cit.*, i, 68, n., 82, 96, 135.

1812, there was not much regret at Pera. He had not, however, gone permanently. Seeing the Golden Horn first at the age of 21, he did not finally turn his back on it until he was 73.

Stratford's successor in 1812 was Liston, under whom the dragomans were finally transferred to the complete jurisdiction of the ambassador. The Treasury was persuaded to introduce an improved salary scale and Liston was glad to be entrusted with its introduction as he regarded himself as the originator, as far back as 1795 when he was a Levant Company servant, of the plan to abolish fees in favour of consolidated salaries. He blamed himself for the hardship the dragomans had experienced and discussed the problems of recruitment and remuneration with Castlereagh before leaving London. He had known Bartholomew Pisani for many years, and the others since they were *giovani*, and thought them "men of ability who have served well, who have sometimes been entrusted with the management of delicate and difficult business, and who upon the whole have constant and full employment". On reaching the Porte, Liston found Bartholomew Pisani still drawing his former salary, although he had been first interpreter since 1800. Recent, inflationary years had led him into debt, and he was proposing to retire on a two-thirds pension and find more lucrative employment in the world of trade for his last working years. Liston was in consternation, telling Castlereagh, "We cannot do without him". Castlereagh eased these apprehensions by paying up much, though not all, the arrears Pisani claimed, and he also sent Chabert compensation for his losses in the 1810 fire. In ordering Liston to take over the dragomans, he told him to allocate one or more to look after commercial business, so it was now the Company which was borrowing from the embassy. The Company continued to pay the salaries, but according to the new scale laid down by the Foreign Office. The first dragoman's salary was quintupled (3,000 piastres to 15,000), other dragoman salaries doubled, and the pittance of the *giovani* quadrupled. When the £400 for the confidential work of the "political" dragoman is added, the interpreter service cost £3,000 a year.[13]

Between Stratford's departure and the arrival of Strangford in 1820, Liston's somnolent interregnum and the quiescence of Eastern affairs stayed the growth of "dragomania" at the Foreign Office; Terrick Hamilton went out but did not supplant Bartholomew Pisani, nor would Strangford take Hamilton into his confidence in the early stages of the Greek crisis. Hamilton was not often used in the capacity of an interpreter either, and Strangford preferred to evolve his opinions

[13] Castlereagh to Liston, 27 March 1812, F.O. 78/79.

and negotiate at the Porte with the assistance of his fifth dragoman, George Wood, regarding whom something must be said at this point.

Wood was that rare thing, a British-born dragoman. He does not appear in Elgin's list of dragomans in 1799, and seems to have been first employed when Elgin was in urgent need of interpreters to serve in Egypt. As British dragoman to the Grand Vezir, and then in the same capacity to the "English in Egypt", Wood sufficiently impressed Elgin with the testimonials he brought back to be sent with a Turkish mission to London shortly afterwards. He fell ill in England, missed the "preferment" Hawkesbury promised him, and returned to Constantinople, where he was relegated for a few years to purely commercial work and the litigation arising from the protection of British mercantile interests in the Ottoman courts. He re-entered the political sphere in 1821, rising suddenly at the expense of all his fellows. He is found conducting an intimate private correspondence with Strangford at the very time Hamilton was complaining to his friend, Robert Gordon, that the ambassador did not show him six despatches a year. Unlike Adair, Strangford evidently kept the key to *his* archives! When Strangford went to the congress of Verona, as second delegate to the Duke of Wellington, he kept in touch with his Austrian colleague to the Porte, Lutzov, and sent the *Reis Efendi* frequent admonitions, through Wood, pleading for Turkey to assist his advocacy of her cause by showing moderation in the suppression of the Greeks.[14] Only Strangford's transference to St Petersburg denied Wood a more lasting enjoyment of the position of "political" dragoman.

Chabert became first dragoman on the retirement of Bartholomew Pisani in 1824, just a year before the winding-up of the Company. About the same time, four new student-interpreters were sworn in. There was no premonition of the demise of the Company until the very last months of its life and even then the earliest speculations regarding service under the Crown were characterized by curiosity rather than apprehension. The dragomans knew they were unpopular at home, and blamed Stratford for it, but they were still confident of their indispensability.[15]

[14] The private papers of Richard Wood, son of George Wood, are in the writer's custody and include a few letters to, and copies of others written by, the father. Hamilton's plaintive letters to Gordon are in the British Museum, Add. MS. 43213.

[15] Canning to George Lidell, 30 May 1825, F.O. 366/348; Wood, *op. cit.*, 199 *et seq.*; according to a memorandum in Foreign Office to Treasury, 21 May 1841, F.O. 78/467, the new *giovani* were Robert Chabert, Henry Simmons, Etienne

Stratford returned to Constantinople in February 1826, and until the signing of the St Petersburgh Protocol, in May, tried very hard to bring the Turks to a realization of their danger, and to effect what, had it succeeded, would have amounted to an eleventh-hour accommodation between them and the Greeks. The Turks did not respond to Stratford; they did react to the Russian ultimatum. Stratford's chances of success were really infinitesimal but he attributed his failure to the fact that his Austrian and Prussian colleagues, Baron Ottenfels and Count Miltitz, counterworked him at the Porte with the active help of his own chief interpreter, Chabert. A letter Stratford received in later years said, "You were uniformly betrayed. All your words were taken down by the Baron at C[habert]'s dictation. Your interviews with the R[eis] E[fendi], in fact all the secrets confided by you, your opinion and views, were every evening registered, and the two villains saw each other and remained till late together." The same letter asserted that Strangford, after his transference to St Petersburg in 1824, kept up a correspondence with Miltitz which must have increased Stratford's difficulties, and that it was from a copy of Crabbe's *Synonyms*, presented to him by Strangford, that Chabert devised the cypher for his shameful transactions with the Prussian minister. Stratford "decided rightly or wrongly that more injury would be done by disgracing the dragoman than by retaining and watching him", but he never trusted him again where diplomatic matters were concerned.[16]

Stratford was replaced in 1829, only to return to Turkey again in 1831 when, in order to negotiate with the Turks most advantageously on the question of the frontiers of the new Greek state, he made a special arrangement for the conduct of confidential work. He selected three agents for his purposes, Dr MacGuffog, Stefanaki Vogorides, and David Urquhart. Each of this trio had important contacts; MacGuffog, the embassy physician, was also medical adviser to the Sultan; Vogorides, the mysterious, anglophile Prince of Samos, had access to the Sultan and the favourites of the Divan;[17] Urquhart, a frantic Russophobe whose views and publications did so much to advance the Turkish cause in Britain, was on good terms with the Grand Vezir. Without being so good a Turkish speaker as he liked to give out, Urquhart hoped a career of dark intrigue, suited to his melodramatic tempera-

Pisani and Richard Wood, and the date of their appointment 28 November 1823. Of Elgin's *giovani*, Calavro became a dragoman in 1800, and Frederick Pisani in 1814; Navon and Aidé had died or retired by 1823.

[16] Lane-Poole, *op. cit.*, i, 406–16.   [17] Lane-Poole, *op. cit.*, i, 506–7.

ment, was unfolding before him.[18] As for Chabert, Stratford "thought
it best to have a frank explanation with him at once. Delicacy was out
of the question; my opinion of his character was no secret. I told him
at our first meeting that it was unchanged; . . . the sole test of his
conduct, in my judgement, would be a success [in the frontier negotia-
tions]; if my ship went down, his boat would infallibly share its fate.
He bowed, and silently accepted the terms."[19] Stratford's ship did not
founder; nor, as a result, did Chabert's boat. Nevertheless, Frederick
Pisani, the third dragoman, replaced Chabert in the conduct of the
embassy's public relations with the Turkish ministers.

Lord Ponsonby became ambassador to Turkey in place of Stratford in
1833, a year in which Russian supremacy in the councils of the Sultan
seemed to have been secured by the sensational treaty of Hunkyar-
Iskelesi.[20] Ponsonby was less austere than Stratford, and positively lax
in matters of embassy routine and administration, but his amiable
exterior concealed a strong will and great diplomatic resource. Chabert
was given no opportunity to restore himself to favour, and the £400
he formerly enjoyed for the performance of the political work now
went entirely to Frederick Pisani. The other dragomans were taken
back into confidence and political employment by 1836, for Ponsonby
used every means he could find to combat Russian influence, and
expected all his staff, *giovani* included, to contribute to the struggle.
When Urquhart came home at the end of 1834 to develop the anti-
Russian thesis which obsessed him, his place among Ponsonby's closest
confidants was filled by Richard Wood, who had just succeeded his
late father as fifth dragoman. Wood soon attained a degree of intimacy
with the ambassador unequalled in this period. He dined regularly with
the Ponsonbys who detested Pera and lived out at Tarabya on the
Bosphorus, shared the ambassador's stratagems and fears, and performed vital missions for him to Syria and Kurdistan.[21] In fact, Wood
and his close friend, Etienne Pisani, helped Frederick Pisani to restore

[18] G. H. Bolsover, "David Urquhart and the Eastern Question", *Journ. Mod.
Hist.*, viii (1936), 444; C. K. Webster, "Urquhart, Ponsonby and Palmerston",
Eng. Hist. Review, lxii (1947), 327; his claim to have "means of communication,
and information wholly distinct from the regular diplomatic routine" is in
Urquhart to Palmerston, 28 February 1834, F.O. 78/249, and the virtual con-
fession that he could not easily dispense with a dragoman is in a letter to Back-
house, 29 September 1835, F.O. 78/266.
[19] Lane-Poole, *op. cit.*, i, 509.
[20] G. H. Bolsover, "Lord Ponsonby", *Slavonic Review*, xiii (1934), 99.
[21] Wood's *Memorandum on his Services in Syria* is in F.O. 78/961; a letter in the
Wood Papers (hereafter W.P.), Ponsonby to Wood, 4 December 1834, shows

to the office of dragoman much of its former stature and importance. It was just about this time, however, when the Levantines were emerging from a period of disrepute, that the plan to anglicize the interpreter service began to take shape at the Foreign Office.

Palmerston discussed the question of reform with Stratford before the latter went East again in 1831, and with Urquhart while he was in England. The Foreign Secretary was rightly dissatisfied with the expedients to which Stratford had found it necessary to resort when he employed MacGuffog and Vogorides; and a situation in which the senior dragoman could not be trusted, while lesser-paid interpreters or complete outsiders who were not in official receipt of any salary at all performed the confidential work, clearly could not be allowed to go on. It was financially wasteful, prejudicial to diplomatic process, and productive of discord and jealousy among the Levantines.[22] In the first instance, Palmerston did not think it very practicable to introduce a scheme for training British personnel, and believed that reform should consist of weeding out incompetents and replacing them with men already available in Pera. Thus his first comment on the subject, scrawled on a memorandum drawn up in 1831, says, "Both Chabert and Pisani [i.e. Antonio, who had been second dragoman since 1800, and who was loyal without being very able] ought to be got rid of", to which is added the very relevant afterthought, "Can more honest successors easily be found?"[23] Palmerston himself thought the answer to his own question was in the negative, and favoured promoting George Wood to be "political" dragoman. Wood's death in 1834 ended that idea, and Urquhart, arriving in England soon after, was

that Wood held an appointment in a Turkish department of state where confidential information was to be had. Ponsonby admits it is "a wholly unusual proceeding"; Wood must "allow the Pera world . . . to talk", and "trust entirely to me to take care that you shall not suffer" at the Foreign Office.

[22] Dragoman salaries at this time are specified in Mandeville to Foreign Office, 1 October 1831, F.O. 366/569. Francis Chabert, £1,100; Antonio Pisani, £500; Frederick Pisani, £300; Calavro, £300; George Wood, £300; the *giovani* Etienne Pisani, Robert Chabert, and Henry Simmons were being paid £80 per annum, while Richard Wood was receiving £110. Chabert's salary was so high because it included the £400 given for "political" work. Part of this £400 had to be surrendered to Frederick Pisani in 1832, and the rest of it later on. It was all going to Pisani by 1842, along with an extra £200 which Ponsonby added to Pisani's salary as from April 1837. Pisani's gross income of £900 in 1842 was almost thrice the salary of an embassy attaché. See Aberdeen to Canning, 24 May 1842, F.O. 78/473.

[23] Palmerston's minute, 19 October 1831, on Hammond's undated *Memorandum*, F.O. 366/569.

able to canalize all further discussion towards the discovery of British replacements for the Levantines. Ponsonby, aloof and jealously protective of the reliable men like Richard Wood and Frederick Pisani, contributed nothing to the discussion from Constantinople, and after his quarrel with Urquhart in 1837 was more than ever disposed to work through men who were serving him well.

The *débâcle* of Hunkyar-Iskelesi, the precariousness of the truce between the Sultan and Muhammad Ali, and the maturing plan to seek a revision of the existing Turkish tariff, all lent point to the dragoman issue, which came to a head in 1838, soon after Urquhart went out to supervise the commercial negotiations with the Ottoman authorities. His parting shot had been typical: "I feel perfectly certain of the failure of the proposal with regard to the Tariff if the negotiations are undertaken through the machinery of the Dragomans."[24] Urquhartian sentiments are also apparent in the memorandum which opened up the whole question in January 1838. It was the work of one Murray, a clerk in the consular department of the Foreign Office. This was only appropriate as it was hoped to transfer at least one or two dragomans to harmless vice-consular posts while recruiting Turkish- or Arabic-speaking Englishmen for the more important stations such as Smyrna and Alexandria. The theme of consular reorganization had been chiefly developed by Colonel Campbell, consul-general in Egypt, and it was suggested that Campbell's ideas might be "made the ground plan of an enlarged system for providing those efficient Services of British Subjects which are required" for the interpreter service too. Murray went on, "A Turkish Minister is known to fear, because he cannot trust, any Dragoman . . . and at the present time a British Minister at Constple [*sic*] cannot be said to have any

[24] For the negotiations, see Webster, *Foreign Policy of Palmerston, 1831–41* (London, 1951), ii, chap. 7; the "failure" predicted by Urquhart did not come to pass, but there were discrepancies between the Turkish and English versions of the Commercial Treaty of 1838 which produced difficulties later on. The Turks claimed the treaty allowed them a salt monopoly at Salonika, the British merchants that it admitted them to the wine trade in Turkey. Pisani may be to blame for the discrepancies, but both Bulwer, who conducted the negotiations on the British side, and Ponsonby were anxious to settle the business quickly. Cartwright, the consul-general, assisted Bulwer in the negotiations, and even if he could not easily follow Pisani's discussions with the Turks, had enough Turkish to check the Turkish version against the English one. In any case, it was Ponsonby's responsibility to see that the two versions tallied. Pisani probably aimed at giving both sides what they wanted, hoping small, and, to him, unimportant differences between the versions would not be noticed; see Stratford Canning to Aberdeen, 24 May 1842, F.O. 78/478.

certain means of ascertaining what are the real sentiments of a Turkish Minister." The implication of this piece of Urquhartism was that Turkish ministers went in fear of their confidential remarks to a British dragoman being repeated to other foreign ministers than the British. It would be different, however, if "Gentlemen of Talent and Education", linguistically qualified, went out as "ostensible and important Members of the Embassy and of His Majesty's Diplomatick Service".[25]

Unfortunately for this ideal, Turkish was not taught in any of the larger schools which prepared youths for the Indian service such as Haileybury and Addiscombe, and, upon enquiry by the Foreign Office, it was found that there was only one person in all London teaching Turkish. Murray, observing that "the study of Eastern Languages . . . appears rarely to have been undertaken for pleasure", suggested that six or eight youths should be sent to learn Greek and Turkish in the lands where they were spoken. After three years of intensive study, they could come back and serve a year in the Foreign Office before taking up their Eastern appointments, whether as consuls, dragomans, or embassy attachés. Palmerston wondered whether men would be found who would undertake the language course without a guarantee of ultimate employment, and did not see how the men, if they went out, could be supervised in their studies. "But I wish very much to get rid of the Dragomans, the employment of and Dependence upon whom is most injurious to our Interests." The disposition of 1831, to find local replacements, had changed by 1838.

Edmund Hammond, a clerk associated with the Turkey department of the Foreign Office, took up specifically the problem of personnel in a further memorandum, arguing that there should be no insuperable difficulty in finding the right candidates to take over as the existing dragomans dropped out of service through death or retirement.[26] Chabert was "advanced in years", Antonio Pisani had served even longer, Calavro had done 42 years and Frederick Pisani 41. "The material point is to secure persons of approved fidelity for the transaction of the confidential business" and this meant "British Subjects upon

[25] Murray's *Memorandum on the Dragoman System in the Levant*, January 1838, with Palmerston's minute of 6 February, F.O. 366/569.

[26] Hammond's *Memorandum respecting Dragomans*, 14 February 1838, and *Further Memorandum*, 25 April 1838, F.O. 366/569. Hammond believed any Oriental language would be useful for a candidate submitting himself for a Turkey interpretership, possibly under the influence of Fox-Strangway's minute of 13 February in which Turkish was described as "a pedantic mixture of Tartar, Arabic and Persian". Such vagueness was not unusual; Palmerston thought Arabic was the language of Persia.

whom entire trust and reliance may be placed, in lieu of Foreigners, upon whom no reliance whatever can be placed". Where did one find them? "English education, and the spirit which pervades our public Schools and Universities, and the general tone of English Society, instil into the mind of a young man those high feelings of honour and of principle which peculiarly distinguish the English character." Hammond did not want the Levantines ousted at once, nor is it easy to see how they could have been. In fact, if the rather despised but plodding second dragoman had died in 1838, while Frederick Pisani was assisting at the commercial negotiations for the revised Tariff, the ostensible as opposed to secret channels of communication with the Porte could hardly have been kept open. Wood was in Syria, Urquhart disgraced, Chabert unemployable, and Calavro dying. Only the *giovani* were left and of these Ponsonby was already employing Etienne Pisani full time. Hammond acknowledged only one real drawback to his proposals; future governments might alter, or revoke completely, any plan of action decided on by Lord Palmerston—"a system established by one Government may in a few years be subverted by another . . . the caprices of an ambassador . . . might render a man, without any fault of his own, unfit for, or might exclude him from employment". Still unconvinced that men would be found to take this occupational risk, Palmerston again shelved the problem, partly, one imagines, because the outbreak of war in the East in 1839, and the international complications proceeding from it, disinclined him to change his horses, however unsatisfactory, in mid-stream.

Action was only taken with the return of peace, and upon the basis of yet another memorandum, this one coming from Alison, the second attaché at Constantinople. Alison, described by Lane-Poole as a "Voltairean *laisser faire* personality" of "subtle and penetrating" mind, was consulted on the advisability of sending out young men to learn Greek and Turkish, and he frankly placed more hope in the increasing knowledge of French among the Turks than in the possibility of producing respectable speakers of Turkish for ourselves. He was, on the other hand, concerned at the number of Frenchmen, Austrians, and Russians finding employment in Turkey on the strength of their competence in Turkish, and for this reason, if for none other, he believed the British Government had no choice but to persevere with the linguistic training of its own nationals. He found five Frenchmen working in official capacities in the office of Resid Paşa, the great advocate of westernization in Turkey, and there were two more in his private household. Britain could not afford to be left behind or to rely for the local maintenance of her influence upon unofficial and unorthodox supporters like Vogorides. If the British Government proposed to make an early decision for the recruitment of English dragomans, Alison wrote, he would guarantee to get them the best available tuition in Turkish and Greek. "I will pledge myself to perform what I have stated, and to spare no pains, with fair stuff to deal with."[27] The matter was quickly settled after this and Hammond, forgetting his usual parsimony, got Palmerston to offer Alison an extra £100 per annum for supervising the progress of the candidates sent out. Overruling Hammond's suggestion that the first two candidates might be got from Rugby, Palmerston invited the Vice-Chancellors of Oxford and Cambridge each to supply a person of promise. After all the talk of British dragomans, one of the first two men selected was the son of the Italian professor of Italian at Cambridge. In 1845, two more students went out, one of whom was Percy Smythe, the gifted son of Stratford's old *bête noire*, Strangford. By 1849 these four men, trained to the satisfaction of Alison in the appropriate tongues, were on the paid staff of the embassy, and usually referred to as the Oriental attachés. The name attaché was regarded as less obnoxious than dragoman and more suited to the dignity of the young Englishmen.[28]

The reaction of the Chaberts and Pisanis to the modification of the old order is not known in any detail, and it is possible that Ponsonby, with his casual ways, encouraged at least some of them to hope that the axe would never fall. Ponsonby was highly satisfied with the contribution of Frederick Pisani to the successful outcome of the Tariff negotiations, and in informing the Foreign Office of the signing of the Commercial Treaty of 1838 wrote, "there is very much due to him for the skill and activity with which he exerted himself". Ponsonby's attitude could not, of course, obscure the fact that his confidential diplomacy on political matters was still being conducted by Vogorides, except when Richard Wood was in Pera between missions, and it was precisely that confidential work which Palmerston wanted in British hands. It might have been allocated almost entirely to Wood, and Stratford tried to tempt him back to it even after his appointment as

[27] Lane-Poole, *op. cit.*, ii, 69; Alison to Hammond, undated, 1841, F.O. 366/569.
[28] Hammond to Palmerston, minute, 9 June 1841, in which Hammond wrote, "I am not a Rugby man myself; but I hear a great deal of the manner in which the Rugby boys distinguish themselves in standing for Scholarships at Oxford"; Palmerston's decision to employ university men is in a minute of 10 June; Palmerston to Vice-Chancellors of Oxford and Cambridge, 21 August 1841, F.O. 366/569. The men selected were Almeric Wood, William Doria (1841); Hon. Percy Smythe, T. F. Hughes (1845).

consul at Damascus in 1841, but having once tasted freedom, Wood was unwilling to return to the city where he had been exposed to Urquhart's humiliations. He knew, in 1842, that Stratford was ready to give him an attachéship if he wanted one; he preferred oblivion, and got it in greater measure than he really expected. Before that, and while his own future as a dragoman was still in doubt, Wood was as anxious as any of his fellows at the obscurity of their prospects, and he discussed his career in letters exchanged with his sailor friend, William Lyon, captain of a merchant vessel trading regularly in Levant waters. Lyon knew the East well and was a hostile critic of the Levantine dragomans, telling Wood, "No one, not even Urquhart, has a worse opinion of our system of Dragomans than I have." He too thought "it certainly would be well to pay several clever young men, and pay them well to learn the Turkish language", and "as you are an Englishman in Blood and Feeling, and as Englishmen alone are to be declared capable of holding the situation of Dragoman, you would rank among the first". In fact, he thought Wood's only serious competitor for the senior appointment was the person from whom he acquired his information of the trend of Foreign Office opinion, Urquhart, "a strange fish, [who] has much talent, but little Ballast". It was a sound nautical judgement, and Lyon was not the only friend who thought Wood was foolish in allowing injured pride to hinder professional advancement.[29]

The degree of Wood's error in choosing a Syrian consulate before a return to the work of the embassy was only made apparent with the passage of time and the discovery that the Levantines were not so superfluous as the Oriental attachés were expected to make them. Contrary to all predictions, the latter did not prove adequate to the tasks of personal negotiation and interpretation, and increasing paper work at the embassy was sufficient to tie them to their desks there and to leave little time or energy for anything else. It is quite startling to discover how many Levantines whose early demise or retirement was predicted in 1841 were still in active service when the Crimean War began, performing their traditional tasks to the exclusion of the Oriental attachés who, by that time, were wholly engaged, along with the diplomatic

[29] W.P., Stratford Canning to Wood, 17 April, Wood to Canning, 30 April 1842. In replying, Wood wrote, "The little consideration attached to the profession of Dragoman, the constant and public attacks made upon the individuals themselves and the little respect they enjoyed in general not only made me anxious to quit it but the moral effect was such as to have induced Lord Ponsonby to employ me abroad in confidential missions"; W.P., William Lyon to Wood, 22 February, 19 November 1836, 4 September 1837.

attachés, in paper work. It had been thought that George Wood's
generation of interpreters, steadily infiltrated by the succeeding one
to which his son belonged, would have disappeared by the mid-forties.
Instead, the growth and spread of embassy duties made it necessary
to promote the *giovani* before the older men died out, and in 1850
there were more Levantine dragomans in simultaneous service than
ever before. Francis Chabert was still first dragoman, and receiving his
salary as such, though devoting his labours exclusively to commercial
affairs; Antonio Pisani, who had served Elgin, was still there as second;
Frederick Pisani was third and "political" dragoman; Robert Chabert
and Etienne Pisani, appointed *giovani* with Richard Wood in 1823,
became dragomans in 1841 when he was nominated to Damascus;
Simmons, a *giovane* with them, was promoted dragoman in 1849.
Count Pisani, after 36 years' service, remained custodian of the
archives although Hammond had deplored such an arrangement
years before.[30]

Also contrary to expectation was the hostility Stratford started to
show towards the Oriental attachés. "It was new and unpleasant for
him to have unknown youngsters thrust upon him by the Foreign
Office, some of whom had no other recommendation than being the
relatives of noblemen who were useful to the government", is his
biographer's explanation,[31] in apparent disregard of the earlier claim
that it was Stratford who suggested the new *régime*, and the abundant
evidence of Lane-Poole's own chapters which show that it was precisely with the "relatives of noblemen" that Stratford got along best.
The biographer was as vague about the categories of attaché as he was
concerning dragomans. Stratford got on well enough with Percy
Smythe, Stanley of Alderley, Lord Napier and Ettrick, Lord Cowley
and Odo Russell; of these, only Smythe was an Oriental attaché. The
other three Oriental attachés were not of noble family, and here the
main complaint was against their health rather than their ancestry:

---

[30] In his *Memorandum* of 14 February 1838, Hammond had written, "If the
system of Dragomans is bad, the system which brings one of the body into the
Chancery and gives him habitual access to the Archives of the Embassy is much
worse." F.O. 366/569; Count Pisani, formerly Alexander Pisani, is sometimes
listed as a *giovane*, but this is because his work in the Chancery prevented his
becoming a dragoman, long after he was linguistically qualified. He never
became a dragoman, but enjoyed higher pay and status than the *giovani*. He went
with Strangford to the congress of Verona in 1822, and was sent in 1833 to advise
Ibrahim, the stepson of Muhammad Ali, not to come nearer to the Porte than
Konya.

[31] Lane-Poole, *op. cit.*, ii, 68.

"they have not a sound constitution among them". Perhaps the real cause of Stratford's dissatisfaction with his diplomatic attachés was their refusal to become infected with his own zeal for Turkish reforms.

When the Holy Places dispute flared up, Stratford was discovering just how much of the burden of embassy work, both diplomatic and clerical, rested on the Levantine dragomans and himself. Pride in his own flawless health made him impatient of illness in others, and while he and the Levantines plodded on, negotiating, wrangling, pleading, and writing endlessly, he came to feel that the attachés, both Oriental and diplomatic, did not pull their weight. "Not one of them is equal to half the fatigue that I endure, and often after the departure of a messenger there is a general occultation of the minor luminaries." The Oriental attachés had, in effect, surrendered to the Levantines their traditional functions and had themselves become the auxiliaries of the diplomatic attachés. The duties of negotiation at the Porte fell squarely upon Frederick Pisani, Etienne Pisani, and Robert Chabert, and when Frederick finally declared himself too infirm for the daily journeys between Pera and the Porte, Stratford expressed "concern at the loss of your more active services".[32]

When the war actually broke out in 1854, it was only too apparent that the dragoman question had not been solved by the reform of 1841. Indeed the situation was deteriorating. Just prior to 1855, Francis Chabert, Antonio Pisani, and Robert Chabert died in swift succession, but because Palmerston had refused, over a period of years, to appoint any more Levantine *giovani*, there was now a dangerous shortage of reserves for the interpreter service. The Oriental attachés, whose numbers had not increased beyond the original four, could not step into the breach, even temporarily. "Mr Wood is unfortunately deceased, Mr Doria and Mr Smythe are all but confirmed invalids, and Mr Hughes, through Your Lordship's kindness, is about to find a more congenial sphere of exertions at Erzerum." Clarendon threw the problem back, enquiring plaintively if more British dragomans were really necessary in light of the vastly increased use of French by the Turks.[33] Stratford needed no more encouragement and reverted frankly and with characteristic independence to the old habit of recruiting local men, Levantine or British, for the interpreterships. His first nominee was the son of a former Turkey merchant called Sarell, but by 1857

[32] Lane-Poole, *op. cit.*, ii, 136; Stratford Canning to Malmesbury, 29 May 1852, F.O. 366/569.

[33] Stratford Canning to Clarendon, 3 June 1856, F.O. 78/1180; Clarendon to Stratford Canning, 13 August 1856, F.O. 78/1165.

some very un-English names were creeping back into the register of dragomans—Stavrides, Revelaki, Alishan.[34] In 1860 another Englishman in the Levant, Alfred Sandison, became a dragoman, apparently by nomination also, and recruitment by civil service examination for the Turkey interpreterships only began in 1877. Then, as the examinations were conducted in London, and British subjects alone could sit for them the days of the Levantine dragoman were numbered.[35]

Stratford left the Porte finally in 1858. In his last years of service, he had become such a partisan of the Levantines that Hammond could write, à propos an increase of salary for them, "I am perfectly prepared for his objecting to them [i.e. the new scales of payment] altogether, first because of his . . . inveterate dislike to the system of Oriental attachés, and secondly because he will feel jealous at a suggestion for the benefit of the Dragomans originating otherwise than from himself." The Levantines did not die very willingly, nor very quickly, and several gave years of service after Stratford's final departure. Frederick Pisani gave intermittent service to the year of his death, 1871. Henry Simmons died within a few weeks of him. Etienne Pisani, "the faithful Etienne" as Stratford called him, retired after the Franco-Prussian war, and died in 1882, stubbornly demonstrating how the climate which removed Palmerston's Oriental attachés preserved the Levantine dragomans who were born to it.

[34] Stratford Canning to Clarendon, 4 May 1857, F.O. 366/569.
[35] Foreign Office List (1878).

SALISBURY AND THE TUNISIAN
QUESTION, 1878-1880[1]

By André Raymond

THE REGENCY of Tunis had been a dependency of the Ottoman
Empire since, at the end of the sixteenth century, the Turkish con-
querors had installed there a pasha and a military force, but in the course
of the seventeenth and eighteenth centuries it had become virtually
autonomous, under the influence first of the Muradite Beys and then
of the Husainite dynasty, which was to occupy the throne of Tunis
without interruption from 1705 to 1957. In the nineteenth century,
Ahmad Bey (1837–55) had struggled stubbornly to obtain recognition
of his semi-independence by the Ottoman Sultan and by the Great
Powers, especially France and England.

While France, established since the capture of Constantine in 1837 on
the very frontiers of Tunisia, was perfectly content with a *de facto*
independence which placed little Tunisia under her influence, Great

---

[1] This essay is mainly based on part of a thesis presented to the University of
Oxford in 1954 for the degree of D.Phil., under the title of "British Policy towards
Tunis, 1830–1881". We should like to take this opportunity of thanking Messrs
C. A. Julien, Professor at the Sorbonne, and F. W. D. Deakin, Warden of St
Antony's College, for enabling us to undertake the present study. We are greatly
indebted to Mr A. H. Hourani, Fellow of St Antony's College, who was our
supervisor, and who, giving us throughout the two years of our study in Oxford
untiring and almost daily help, enabled this work to be completed.

Thanks to the kindness of the Rt Hon. the Marquis of Salisbury, and the
Librarian of Christ Church, Oxford, we were subsequently able to consult the
Salisbury Papers, to which it was not possible to have access during the writing
of the thesis. We should like to thank the Marquis of Salisbury also for allowing
us to quote from the papers in the present essay. By recourse to these documents
it has been possible to clear up a certain number of points and to acquire a more
direct knowledge of Salisbury's diplomatic methods and aims. The doubts which
remain (in particular about the crucial period April–August 1878) could not be
cleared up except by consulting Cabinet papers, to which of course there is no
access.

Britain had tried for nearly half a century to consolidate the bonds, entirely theoretical, which still linked Tunisia to the Ottoman Empire. The English attitude was motivated by the desire both to prevent France from extending her Algerian possessions towards Tunisia, and to maintain "the integrity of the Ottoman Empire", which had become one of the dogmas of British politics since Pitt, Canning and, above all, Palmerston. With this end in view the Foreign Office and the consuls of Great Britain in Tunis (the last in date, Sir Richard Wood, had been appointed in 1856) waged a long war to maintain the *status quo* there.

This policy came up against a certain number of obstacles which were in the end to prove insurmountable. First of all, it was impossible to persuade the Beys to acquiesce in having their status as quasi-independent sovereigns called in question again. This was perfectly clear in the time of Ahmad Bey: the "French danger", tirelessly denounced by English agents in Tunis, but against which he could always invoke the aid of Great Britain, must have appeared to him as infinitely less dangerous than the clumsy efforts of the Ottomans to re-impose a more effective authority in Tunis. In any case, Turkey, a protector whose intentions were doubtful, was powerless to fulfil the role assigned to her by British diplomacy, on account of the weakness which she manifested throughout the "Eastern crises" of the nineteenth century. In the event, French pressure (in the guise of protection offered to the Bey against too enterprising a suzerain) was to prove the more irresistible in that at no moment does Britain seem to have contemplated replying to it by force.

By about 1869, therefore, Tunisia was in fact a principality nearly independent of the Porte, except for some outward signs by which Ottoman suzerainty was still affirmed. The creation in that year of an International Commission of the Debt and the institution of foreign control over the finances of Tunisia, driven to bankruptcy by the imprudence of her rulers and the greed of her European money-lenders, seemed at the time likely to prevent the establishment of an exclusive French guardianship. But when France was put out of action by her defeat in 1871, the Commission helped in the event to safeguard the future of French enterprises and, for the present, to limit the development of Italy's entirely new ambitions. The attempt made in 1871, with British support, to establish firmer links between Tunisia and the Ottoman Empire, with a view to weakening French influence, was devoid of practical results, for neither France nor Italy was willing to recognize the imperial firman obtained at Istanbul by Khair al-Din.

Moreover, the Ottomans were becoming too involved in their own difficulties to take over this distant dependency.

Between 1873 and 1876 there was a lull in this gradual collapse of Tunisia, threatened on all sides by the ambitions of the great European imperialism which often took the form of economic penetration. Under the authority of an upright and clear-sighted minister, Khair al-Din, the internal situation of Tunisia improved; at the same time the establishment of English enterprises in the economic sphere was to help to neutralize the hostile pressure of France and Italy. Nevertheless, this balance did not prove lasting. The British Consul did not receive much support from his government, which had no important political interests in Tunisia; he did not succeed in interesting English capital in the development of Tunisia, which thus became a closed field of Franco-Italian rivalry.[2] France herself, emerging from the reserve imposed on her by circumstances, assumed again from 1874 a more active political role, encouraged in this by Bismarck, who saw with satisfaction the French turning away from their wounds of 1871 to think about colonial expansion. "It is not for us . . . a disadvantage, nor a tendency to be fought, that French policy is seeking in North Africa a field for her activity," he wrote as early as January 1875 to Hohenlohe.[3] Caught between the contradictory demands of the Powers, Khair al-Din had to relinquish office in July 1877. The Tunisian resistance to French and Italian enterprises was considerably weakened by this, and the Regency began once more to slide down the slope which was to lead to the loss of her independence.

In increasingly marked contrast with the "interventionism" of Consul Wood, the Foreign Office had abstained from adopting an active policy in Tunisia during these years. By claiming as its sole object the maintenance of the political existence of the Regency and by refusing to be mixed up in the internal affairs of the country and in the rivalries of the Powers for predominance, the Foreign Office could not but give the impression that it accepted British effacement in Tunis. British prestige and influence in Tunis, however, remained unique: while the attitude of France and Italy in the seventies had become increasingly hostile, the conciliatory behaviour of England and her readiness to assist the Bey in his difficulties confirmed the traditional disinterestedness of English policy. Wood, who had been Consul in Tunis for more than twenty years, remained a valued adviser of the

---

[2] See our article on "Les tentatives anglaises de pénétration économique en Tunisie (1856–1877)", *Revue Historique*, 1955.

[3] *Politique Extérieure de l'Allemagne* (P.E.A.), Vol. I, January 10, 1875.

Bey and his followers, with whom he entertained intimate relations. At the same time the part which Great Britain played as the centre of resistance to the preponderance of another Power in Tunis remained decisive: Great Britain had played this part quite successfully from 1869 to 1875 against French or Italian ambitions. As long as Great Britain held fast to the policy which Palmerston had defined in 1835, an equilibrium was possible in Tunis between the three Powers.

From the very beginning of the Eastern crisis of 1875–8 rumours respecting projects of partition involving Tunis had been in the air and had reached Tunis. In 1876 Wood reported the uneasiness created by rumours about the intention of Italy to take possession of the Regency if events in the east should lead to the partition of the Turkish provinces in Europe by Russia and Austria. And in December 1877 the French Consul likewise alluded to a German project to transfer Bizerta to Germany or Italy. These reports were however rather conjectural and even if there were some signs that Germany was favouring such schemes of partition, there was no indication at the end of 1877 that Great Britain had in any way changed her traditional policy towards Tunis.

1. *The Eastern Crisis*

The fate of the Regency was sealed during the Eastern crisis of 1875–8. Tunis had never been directly concerned with the international difficulties which were confronting the Ottoman Empire, but the decisions which affected her were a kind of "by-product" of the settlement of the crisis. Two sets of causes explain how the Great Powers came to involve Tunis ultimately in their diplomatic game: firstly the Bismarckian policy of "compensations", which aimed at solving European difficulties at the expense of Turkey by a peaceful redistribution of some of the Ottoman dominions between the Powers interested, and especially between the then most antagonistic Powers, Russia and Great Britain; and secondly the British policy of the "place of arms" which was conceived by Disraeli as a part of his pro-Turk and anti-Russian policy, but which Salisbury was later to change into something not very different from the Bismarckian policy of compensations.[4]

[4] This account of the Eastern Crisis is mainly based upon R. W. Seton-Watson, *Disraeli, Gladstone and the Eastern Question* (London, 1935), William L. Langer, *European Alliances and Alignments* (New York, 1950) and Pierre Renouvin, *Histoire des Relations Internationales*, Vol. VI, part 2 (Paris, 1955), and for the Tunisian point of view upon William L. Langer, "The European Powers and the French Occupation of Tunis" (1878–81) in *American Historical Review*, October 1925 and January 1926.

From the very beginning of the crisis, Bismarck was thinking of the best ways to avoid an extension of the war in Europe: if the Powers did not agree to maintain the territorial *status quo*, the German Chancellor considered that they should work together to maintain the peace of Europe "by amicably settling what should be done with Turkey to satisfy the Powers concerned, instead of going to war about it".[5] "La Turquie tout entière," he wrote to Schweinitz in October 1875, "ne vaut pas que des peuples civilisés d'Europe se détruisent mutuellement pour elle."[6] The problem was to persuade the Powers, and particularly Russia and Great Britain whose policies were most likely to clash in the Balkans and the Near East, to reach a compromise and to accept a settlement based on partition of the Ottoman Empire. Such a policy of partition had been first sketched at Reichstadt in July 1876, when Austria and Russia had provided for a possible partition of the spoils, in case Turkey should be defeated by Serbia and Montenegro. But Bismarck's ideas went much further and tended to involve all the great Powers in the territorial redistribution: his first offers to Great Britain (in the autumn of 1876) were vaguely formulated and sometimes contradictory. While the shares of Russia and Austria were clearly to be Bessarabia and Bosnia-Herzegovina respectively, the Chancellor only hinted at the creation of a British zone of influence in Syria and Egypt (possibly with French co-operation). But he had obviously not yet made up his mind whether France and Italy were to take part in the redistribution, and if so where; although he had begun in 1874 and 1875 to think of directing French action towards colonial enterprises especially in Tunis, he was anxious to avert the possible opposition of Italy to Austrian designs in the Balkans and had joined with Andrassy in the offer of Tunis to Italy (in August and October 1876). Germany had few direct interests in the Mediterranean; but the Mediterranean question was for Bismarck a pawn on the diplomatic chess-board, it could serve as a make-weight in those Bismarckian diplomatic combinations which could, according to circumstances, include France or Italy.

Bismarck's successive offers, however, met with a cold reception in Great Britain: besides Derby's insuperable suspicion and his fear of being duped by Bismarck, a feeling which was shared by many European statesmen at that time, the Foreign Secretary was apprehensive lest such a policy should end in the breaking up of the Ottoman

[5] Langer, *European Alliances and Alignments*, p. 80, Russell to Derby, February 19, 1875.

[6] Quoted in J. Bardoux, *Quand Bismarck dominait l'Europe* (Paris, 1953), p. 70.

Empire, an event which British diplomacy, still clinging to the policy of the *status quo* in the Near East, refused to contemplate. New happenings, such as the opening of the Suez Canal, which shifted commercial and strategic routes to Egypt, and the obvious incapacity of the Ottomans to arrest the course of their decline, certainly discouraged the English from supporting a State which seemed to be about to collapse of its own accord. As early as 1875, Odo Russell, in Berlin, confided to Bismarck that England had completely abandoned her traditional policy in the Eastern question. The "Bulgarian atrocities" had also contributed to the ruin of Turkish credit in Great Britain, to such an extent that Derby stated at this time that if Russia declared war on Turkey, the English government considered it practically impossible to take part in the defence of the Ottoman Empire.[7] But the Foreign Office did not seriously propose to abandon its Turkish policy. In these circumstances, whenever a feeler was put out in Berlin about a policy of compensations, Derby invariably ignored it. Bismarck's first serious proposal was made in November 1876 when Salisbury passed through Berlin on his way to Constantinople, where he was to attend the International Conference about the Balkan crisis. The Chancellor was not confident of the success of the Conference and, Salisbury reported, was "only occupied with settling what shall be done when the Turkish Empire comes in pieces: Bosnia and the Herzegovina for Austria; Egypt for us; Bulgaria possibly for Russia".[8] Salisbury ignored Bismarck's suggestion. As for Derby, he was above all preoccupied by the effect which Bismarck's proposals were likely to have in France: "It is evidently useless to say that we don't want Egypt and don't intend to take it," he wrote to Lord Lyons on December 6, 1876, "I have no doubt that everybody out of France would be glad that we should seize the country. Russia would like it, as making us an accomplice in her plans. Germany would like it still more, as ensuring our being on uncomfortable terms with France for some years to come."[9]

The Foreign Office gave the same reserved answer to Nubar Pasha's overtures about the sale of Egypt by Turkey in April 1877.[10] Bismarck, however, took advantage of these offers to renew his overtures on a

[7] J. Ganiage, *Les Origines du Protectorat Français* (Paris, 1959), pp. 492–3.

[8] G. Cecil, *Life of Salisbury* (London, 1921), Vol. II, p. 97. See also E. Bourgeois, *Manuel de politique étrangère* (Paris, 1906–25), Vol. III, p. 805.

[9] Lord Newton, *Lord Lyons* (London, 1913), Vol. II, p. 105.

[10] P.E.A., Vol. II, Herbert von Bismarck to Bülow; Seton-Watson, *Disraeli, Gladstone and the Eastern Question*, p. 226.

much larger scale. The Chancellor, Odo Russell reported on May 19, 1877, wanted to divert the thought of the Powers from Germany and awaken their interest in the redistribution of power in Turkey:

"To England he has already recommended the occupation of Egypt . . . he has since expressed his anxious hope that England may be some day induced to add Syria, Crete, Cyprus etc. . . . to her eastern possessions. To Austria he has said in confidence that she would do wisely to annex Bosnia and Herzegovina. . . . Italy he is not much inclined to favour but would not object to her acquiring a portion of Tripoli if necessary. France, he says, has already taken possession of her inheritance in the shape of Algeria, but he would help her to add Tunis if France would divert her thoughts from Germany and revenge for the next few years." [11]

Bismarck's policy was probably less tortuous than was commonly thought: deeply concerned by the prospect of a Russian-English clash, the Chancellor sincerely desired to avert it and bring about an understanding.[12] But once more the Foreign Office did not appear to listen to his suggestions; the deepest suspicion continued to prevail in London and above all Disraeli feared lest an attack on the *status quo* in Egypt should lead to a lengthy estrangement from France.[13]

Meanwhile, with the failure of the Constantinople Conference, the rejection by Turkey of the London protocol (March 31, 1877), and ultimately the Russian declaration of war on Turkey (April 24), the situation in the Near East had greatly worsened. The deterioration, to Bismarck's mind, was likely to hasten the collapse of the Ottoman Empire, and this would clear the way for the programme of partition which he regarded as the most satisfactory solution of the entire problem. But for the moment it provoked a stiffening of Disraeli's attitude: the Cabinet, in spite of its internal dissensions, decided that war should be declared on Russia if the Russians occupied Constantinople (July 21).

[11] Winifred Taffs, *Lord Odo Russell* (London, 1938), p. 194.

[12] Langer, *op. cit.*, p. 123. Bismarck, however, defined it at the same time as an object of his policy to "séparer l'Angleterre de la France par la question de l'Egypte et de la Méditerranée". Cf. memorandum of June 15, 1877, quoted in V. Caragiale, *Le Politique des Grandes Puissances et la Question d'Egypte* (Geneva, 1947), p. 21.

[13] "Prince Bismarck would probably like us to seize Egypt as it would be giving a great slap in the face of France," Victoria wrote on July 17, 1877. "What *we intend* to do we shall do *without* Prince Bismarck's permission." Cf. *The Letters of Queen Victoria*, Second Series (London, 1926-8), Vol. II, p. 550.

Given Disraeli's policy of resistance to Russian advance towards the Straits, it was soon apparent that Great Britain needed a centre of action from which she could efficiently defend Constantinople. Colonel Home, who had been sent to Constantinople in 1876 to observe the works of defence, had suggested in January 1877 that the Dardanelles or Cyprus would be a suitable place of arms for that purpose.[14] The Russian declaration of war, and in the autumn the Russian advance in the Balkans and Asia Minor, strengthened Disraeli's position and the military preparations which the Cabinet undertook impressed forcibly upon the Ministers the desirability of occupying a place of arms in the Levant where British forces could be gathered in safety. In November 1877 Disraeli broached the subject with Layard, connecting it with the possibility of consenting to a loan to the Turkish Government: "Some assistance might be afforded to the Porte, if we could contrive to purchase some territorial station conducive to British interests." Disraeli's choice was not yet fixed: "anything in the Mediterranean might excite general jealousy" and a port in the Black Sea would create difficulties because of the Straits Treaties, he wrote to Layard.[15] But by the end of 1877 all the elements which were later to lead to the acquisition of Cyprus had been introduced. The final choice would be determined by diplomatic considerations, and by the desire to establish a commanding position from which both the Dardanelles and the Suez Canal could be watched and guarded.[16]

While the idea of the place of arms was thus gaining in precision, the influence of Lord Salisbury was increasingly felt in the management of foreign affairs—so much so that it gradually superseded that of the titular Minister, the timid and inactive Derby. Salisbury brought with him new conceptions which were gaining ground in the Cabinet. The collapse of Turkey was inevitable: "that the machine here can stand very long, I believe to be impossible", he wrote after the Constantinople Conference. "Even if Russia does not invade, it will crumble of itself."[17] A little later, at the time when he took over the Foreign Office, he seemed to regret that the collapse which he had foreseen had not in fact taken place:

"Much difficulty would have been removed if the Ottoman Empire had gone to pieces in the course of this war and the task of building

[14] D. E. Lee, *Great Britain and the Cyprus Convention* (London, 1934), pp. 37–8.
[15] G. E. Buckle, *Life of Benjamin Disraeli* (London, 1920), Vol. VI, p. 252, Disraeli to Layard, November 22, 1877.
[16] D. E. Lee, *op. cit.*, p. 68.
[17] Seton-Watson, *op. cit.*, p. 137.

a new structure on cleared land had been the one which the European Powers had had to perform. But this has not been the course of events."[18]

In these circumstances there was no point in clinging any longer to Palmerston's outmoded policy: "The old policy . . . of defending English interests by sustaining the Ottoman dynasty has become impracticable," he wrote to Lord Lytton on March 9, 1877. "I think that the time has come for defending English interests in a more direct way by some territorial rearrangement."[19] He defined his ideas about the future of the Turkish Empire in the letter of April 10, 1878, quoted above: "The Turkish Empire still subsists. . . . It is therefore necessary to make it, at all events, tolerably independent, within its reduced proportions and therefore to push the Slav powers behind the Balkans." To some extent Salisbury agreed here with Disraeli's preoccupation of securing a place of arms for Great Britain, but he started from opposite premises, and the views at which he arrived in 1877 were not very different from Bismarck's policy of compensations.

The notion of a general redistribution of territories at Turkey's expense was thus finding new supporters, but its practical realization still came up against great difficulties at the end of 1877. Bismarck's suggestion of Egypt to Great Britain raised serious objections because of French opposition; and a Mediterranean partner remained to be found.

At first sight Italian claims to participation seemed to be more consistent than French: while the French Government remained faithful to the policy of *recueillement*, and appeared to be averse to any far-reaching modification of the *status quo* in the East, Italy had already offered herself as a candidate. The offers made by Austria after the Reichstadt conference had been received with reserve in Rome, but they had given rise to persistent rumours about the intention of Italy to take Tunis in the event of a partition of Turkey-in-Europe by Russia and Austria. During the autumn of 1877 Crispi made a tour of the European capitals, probably to sound the opinion of the various Foreign Offices with regard to possible Italian compensation in the Eastern question. Crispi was not altogether successful in Berlin: Bismarck resented the irredentist tendencies of the Italian Government and refused to contemplate an arrangement in the Alps (Trentino, Istria). "Take Albania," he said and added that he was "ready to treat

[18] *Salisbury Papers* (S.P.), Berlin Drafts, 1878–80, Salisbury to Odo Russell. April 10, 1878.   [19] Cecil, *op. cit.*, Vol. II, p. 130.

[with Italy] against France, but not against Austria".[20] In London Crispi was given the same hint: "Take Albania," Derby said, and Crispi further reports that the Foreign Secretary raised no objection when Crispi alluded to the Italian claim to a compensation in the Alps if Austria should occupy a Turkish province.[21] All this was still confused and not altogether satisfactory for the Italians, whose interest was focused on the Italian provinces which were still in Austria's hands; but it is interesting to note that when, in December 1877, Derby denied any intention of annexing Egypt, he remarked that "Italy would see it a precedent and a justification for seizing Tunis", which seems to indicate that in Derby's "forecast of international brigandage Tunis . . . was allotted to Italy", and not to France.[22]

The last stages of the Russo-Turkish war, the rapid advance of Russian troops towards the Straits, and the signature of the Protocol of Andrinople (January 31, 1878) brought the plans which had been under consideration in 1877 to maturity. Convinced that war was nearly unavoidable, Disraeli undertook to strengthen the British position in the face of Russia by finding partners on the Continent and going ahead with the project of a place of arms. In January overtures were made to Austria, who refused to commit herself, and to France. The moment seemed to be appropriate for a move in Paris: the Dufaure Cabinet, formed in December 1877, had brought to the Quai d'Orsay Waddington who favoured a rapprochement with Great Britain and Germany. The proposal which was made by the Foreign Office to come to an agreement about Oriental questions met, however, with reserve in Paris: the French Government kept the attitude of caution which had been maintained since the beginning of the crisis. It is also very likely that, in spite of Derby's and Disraeli's repeated denials in December 1877 and January 1878, the French Government still felt suspicious about British designs on Egypt. It is, however, perfectly true that if the idea of occupying Egypt had been contemplated by Disraeli, he had now given it up: when the problem of the place of arms was raised in the Cabinet at the end of February 1878, and the decision taken "provisionally" to occupy a station in the east of the Mediterranean in the event of any action (March 8), the points suggested were Mytilene, Saint Jean d'Acre, or a port on the Persian Gulf.[23]

[20] F. Crispi, *Memoirs of Francesco Crispi* (London, 1912), Vol. II, pp. 35–6 and 44.
[21] Crispi, *op. cit.*, p. 73. Seton-Watson, *op. cit.*, p. 477, however, states that "from Derby [Crispi] received the warning that Italy must not hope for compensation in the Eastern Question".
[22] Newton, *op. cit.*, Vol. II, p. 105.   [23] Buckle, *op. cit.*, Vol. VI, p. 253.

At this stage, Disraeli brought before the Cabinet a project of a "Mediterranean League", which was to play the part which the Foreign Office had unsuccessfully ascribed to Austria and France in January. "The Cabinet will launch the League with Italy and Greece alone, if the other Mediterranean Powers decline", Disraeli wrote to Queen Victoria on March 8, 1878. "We count as such France and Austria. If the league is floated, they will soon join."[24] On March 13, Derby accordingly instructed Paget to sound the Italian Government whether they would be willing to enter into an understanding with Great Britain for the maintenance of "their commercial and political interests in the Mediterranean and the Straits".[25] According to Giolitti the price of Italian co-operation was to be Tunis.[26] Unfortunately the Depretis Cabinet, which had appeared favourable to an agreement with Great Britain, had just been overthrown on March 9, 1878; the Cairoli and Corti Government which took its place were mainly preoccupied with their claims north of the Adriatic and disliked the idea of getting into trouble with France by an expansion in the Mediterranean. Derby's offers met with a plain refusal in Rome: The Italian Government, Corti explained to Paget, were "most anxious to act with Her Majesty's Government as far as possible in support of their mutual interests", but they wanted "to avoid if possible being mixed up in complications", and they would not be willing "to bind themselves by any engagement which might perhaps lead them into war".[27]

By this negative answer Italy withdrew from the diplomatic game which was to lead to the partition of the Turkish spoils. In the meanwhile, Bismarck had likewise arrived at the conclusion that it was impossible to rely on the hesitant Italian policy: the Italian Government, which had just rejected new Austrian offers of co-operation (with Tunis as a compensation for Italy)[28] and were falling back into the deadly sin of irredentism, could not be a partner to Germany. On the contrary the Dufaure-Waddington Government gave unmistakable proofs of their desire to favour a rapprochement with Germany.[29] As

[24] *Ibid.*, p. 255.

[25] Public Record Office, F.O. 45/333, Derby to Paget, March 13, 1878.

[26] G. Giolitti, *Memoirs of my Life* (London, 1923), p. 119; and Crispi, *op. cit.*, Vol. II, p. 95.

[27] F.O. 45/337, Paget to Derby, March 28, 1878.

[28] L. Chiala, *Pagine di Storia Contemporanea* (Turin, 1892), Vol. II, p. 346, and A. Giaccardi, *La Conquista di Tunisi* (Milan, 1940), p. 43.

[29] The nomination of Saint Vallier as French Ambassador in Berlin marked the beginning of the "détente". Cf. E. Bourgeois and G. Pagès, *Les Origines de la Grande Guerre* (Paris, 1921), p. 181.

early as the end of February 1878, Bismarck again suggested to the Prince of Wales to "take or occupy Egypt and perhaps Crete", and assured him that he would "find means" to prevent France from quarrelling with England about Egypt.[30] In the course of March 1878 Germany and England were thus similarly led to contemplate making a deal with France and not Italy; but it remained to find the means of inducing France to give up her attitude of *recueillement* and take an active part in the settlement of European questions. Derby's resignation on March 27 and Salisbury's accession to the Foreign Office gave the British Government the means to resolve a diplomatic situation which had now become much clearer.

2. *Salisbury and the Policy of Compensations*

Salisbury had played an active part in the execution of British foreign policy throughout the period, beginning in February 1878, when Derby, depressed by the development of a policy which he disliked, was more and more thinking of resigning and was confining himself to negative action. Salisbury had overcome his first hesitation and given full support to Disraeli's energetic policy towards Russia; but he was above all anxious to avert war, and to find the way towards an agreement with Russia. As Disraeli's faith in the integrity of Turkey had been seriously shaken, Salisbury suggested not questioning the whole San Stefano treaty but concentrating on the problems which were of direct concern to Great Britain: limitation of the Slav States to the Balkan Mountains, freedom of passage through the Straits, and acquisition of two naval stations (Lemnos and Cyprus)[31]—a policy which on the whole was not so far from Gladstone's. With Salisbury in the Foreign Office, a general arrangement on the bases which had been repeatedly suggested by Bismarck since 1876, and successively rejected by Derby, was now possible.

Salisbury first solved the problem of the occupation of a "place of arms" which had caused Derby's resignation. Disraeli had suggested the occupation by Indian troops of two positions in the Levant (probably Cyprus and Alexandretta).[32] At the beginning of April Salisbury informed Layard that a new policy was under discussion regarding an eventual compensation. Egypt (or Syria) was impossible on account of the opposition which France had expressed very clearly again and again (most lately in Waddington's circular note of March 7, 1878).

---

[30] Sir Sidney Lee, *King Edward VII*, Vol. I, p. 432.
[31] Cecil, *op. cit.*, Vol. II, p. 214, Salisbury to Beaconsfield, March 21, 1878.
[32] Buckle, *op. cit.*, Vol. VI, pp. 262–3.

At the beginning of April Salisbury was still doubtful as to the choice to be made. The Russian threat, he wrote to Odo Russell on the 10th, "must be met either by Russia giving up the country acquired or suffering us to acquire some port which would safeguard our Asiatic interests. It may be an island, it may be some place on the West of Asia Minor."[33] Cyprus was definitely chosen between April 18 and May 10, probably on the basis of Colonel Home's memorandum which concluded in favour of the occupation of the island.[34] "If Cyprus be conceded to Your Majesty by the Porte," Disraeli wrote to Queen Victoria on May 5, 1878, "and England, at the same time, enters into a defensive alliance with Turkey, guaranteeing Asiatic Turkey from Russian invasion, the power of England in the Mediterranean will be absolutely increased in that region, and Your Majesty's Indian Empire immensely strengthened. Cyprus is the key of Western Asia."[35] On May 10, Salisbury wrote to Layard about a plan to make a defensive alliance with Turkey on two conditions: internal administrative improvements and cession of Cyprus if the Russians should keep their Armenian conquests.[36] Should Turkey refuse, Salisbury wrote on May 24, Great Britain would abandon her, "and the capture of Constantinople and partition of [the] Empire [would] be the immediate result". In the meantime Salisbury had started conversations with Shuvalov in order to settle Anglo-Russian difficulties before the opening of the Congress, and on May 7 Shuvalov left for Russia with British proposals.

If Italian inability to provide a suitable partner in March 1878 had made England feel the need of obtaining French co-operation very strongly, Salisbury's large-scale plans made it even more important. Waddington appeared willing that France should play an important part in European diplomacy, but, owing to his hostility to any breach of the Mediterranean *status quo*, it was to be feared that British projects would meet with some opposition in France. In fact, Disraeli's first overture to d'Harcourt ("Nous pouvons être obligés de prendre certaines mesures pour la protection de nos intérêts," he told him on April 4. "Nous espérons que la France ne s'en inquiètera pas"), though accompanied by a formal assurance regarding Egypt, was received with reserve:[37] France, Waddington answered on April 8, was above

---

[33] S.P., Berlin Drafts, 1878–80, Salisbury to Odo Russell, April 10, 1878.
[34] D. E. Lee, *op. cit.*, pp. 77–80.
[35] Buckle, *op. cit.*, Vol. VI, p. 291.   [36] D. E. Lee, *op. cit.*, pp. 82–3.
[37] *Documents Diplomatiques Français* (D.D.F.), first series, Vol. II, d'Harcourt to Waddington, April 5, 1878.

S.A.P.—H

all anxious to maintain the *status quo* in the Mediterranean and would regret "une prise de possession quelconque" which would modify it.[38] In fact the French Government was above all preoccupied with seeing Egypt excluded from the discussions which were being prepared. "The goodwill of France depends upon our not acting independently of her in Egypt," Lyons wrote to Salisbury on April 9. "Waddington is himself particularly sensitive about Egypt. The question of occupations is a ticklish one, and I took care not to dwell upon it." But from this point of view the French minister could rest completely assured; the idea of occupying Egypt had already been abandoned in England, and so nothing could hinder a co-operation between the two countries in the Mediterranean. "Under existing circumstances," replied Salisbury to Lyons on April 10, "our interests decidedly point to a hearty co-operation with France in Egyptian matters."[39]

Salisbury's second step was a decisive one. On April 12 he met Münster, the German ambassador, and reminded him of Bismarck's proposal "that England should find her compensation for the Russian advance in Egypt";[40] financial difficulties and French opposition, Salisbury continued, "would make such a mode of restoring British influence inadmissible". Münster made no difficulties about giving the answer which Salisbury was apparently looking for: the difficulties were exaggerated, and France, he asserted, "wished only, or at any rate chiefly, for the harbour of Bona in Tunis, the ancient Carthage" [*sic*]. "The conversation was not pursued," Salisbury concluded.[41] There was no need to say more; the two interlocutors had understood each other *à demi-mot*. Salisbury knew that Bismarck's previous proposals remained valid, that on these bases he could look for an agreement with Russia (this was the object of a second conversation with Münster on April 18), and that the French "indemnification" would be secured at the expense of the Bey of Tunis.

There is no doubt that towards the middle of April 1878, Salisbury had made up his mind and had decided upon abandoning Tunis to

---

[38] D.D.F., Vol. II, Waddington to d'Harcourt, April 8, 1878.

[39] S.P., France, 1878, Lyons to Salisbury, April 9, 1878; and Paris Drafts, 1878–80, Salisbury to Lyons, April 10.

[40] The idea of taking Egypt as a compensation had already been given up in England: Salisbury was thus playing an underhand game with Bismarck who for his part continued to offer Egypt to England, perhaps to embroil her with France. See A. C. Coolidge, *The Origins of the Triple Alliance* (New York, 1926), p. 197, and W. Taffs, *op. cit.*, pp. 218–20. About Bismarck's offers see S.P., Germany, 1878–80, Odo Russell to Salisbury, April 14, 1878.

[41] F.O. 64/899, Salisbury to Odo Russell, April 12, 1878.

France if necessary, as her share in the system of compensations to which the settlement of the Eastern crisis was going to give rise. This meant giving up the Tunisian policy which the Foreign Office had pursued for 50 years and which was primarily based upon the protection of the Regency against French designs.[42] In the absence of any written evidence[43] one may suppose that, having given up the Palmerstonian policy regarding the Ottoman Empire, Salisbury had no scruples about repudiating the traditional British attitude in Tunis, which was part of it, in as far as such a sacrifice, which cost Britain nothing in the Regency, where she had no political interest, was needed for the furtherance of British major interests in the Near East—as Salisbury understood them. The repeated German proposals had made the idea of a system of compensation involving Tunis a very natural one. The abandonment of Tunis was the result of a calculated study of the Mediterranean question and the conclusion of a logical sequence of events which had begun in 1876 and culminated in April 1878 with the decision to occupy Cyprus. On the other hand, the history of Tunis since 1830 and Roustan's increased activity since 1876 proved that a suggestion about the Regency was not likely to be ignored by the French Government.

On May 11, 1878 (the day after his letter informing Layard of the proposed Anglo-Turkish agreement), Salisbury wrote to Lyons and suggested possible compensations to soothe French feeling against the Mediterranean bargain which was in preparation. Was there any truth, he asked, in the rumour (alluded to by Münster in April) that the eyes of French statesmen were turned towards Tunis? "It is of course an extension of French territory and influence of which we should not have the slightest jealousy or fear." But, Salisbury cautiously added, "I am not assuming in any way that the Porte would wish to give it up. I should only like to have your opinion how far France would wish to have it."[44] Lyons' answer was somewhat sceptical: "I have never

[42] The word "Tunis" had already been mentioned in conversations between French and English diplomats. As early as 1876, during a conversation bearing on the disruption of the Ottoman Empire, Lord Odo Russell had broached the subject with Gontaut Biron: "Pour nous, dit Lord Odo en riant, nous sommes prêts pour le cas d'effondrement! Nous avons mis la main sur l'Egypte! Quant à vous Français, j'imagine que la Tunisie pourrait bien vous aller! Je ne dis pas non, repris-je sur le même ton . . ." (Gontaut-Biron to Decazes, Berlin, April 15, 1876, quoted by J. Ganiage, *op. cit.*, p. 507). But it was probably not meant to be taken seriously.

[43] The Salisbury Papers do not show whether there was a discussion within the Foreign Office or the Government about the new Tunisian policy.

[44] S.P., France Drafts, 1878–80, Salisbury to Lyons, May 11, 1878.

found that the acquisition of Tunis recommended itself to French imagination. . . . [The French] certainly desire that the *status quo* may be maintained in the Mediterranean." The weight of the Ambassador's reserve was, however, greatly lessened by the fact that it was based on the assumption that Salisbury was suggesting exchanging Tunis for Egypt or Syria ("I don't believe [Tunis] would be taken as anything like a set off against English acquisitions in Egypt or Syria").[45] This was no longer the case, as Salisbury remarked in the middle of the month, handing over to Lyons a copy of a private letter to Layard: "You will see that we have deferred to W. views by turning the eyes of desire away from Syria." A few days later Salisbury, coming back to this question, tried to show the logical character of the English position in the face of every French objection. France being hostile to any action, Great Britain was reduced to being single-handed in Asia, and had therefore to take precautions: "We cannot turn the Russians out by ourselves and . . . abandoned by our ally . . . we have no device except to mount guard over the endangered territory and take up the positions requisite for doing so with effect. I do not see what answer the French would have."[46]

Anyhow, it was now too late to retreat: Shuvalov had come back from Saint Petersburg on May 22 and a protocol had been agreed upon as early as the 24th, foreseeing the Russian acquisition of Bessarabia, Kars and Batum; this made it "necessary" for England to protect the Ottoman Empire by a British guarantee of all the Asiatic provinces of Turkey. Cyprus was the price of that guarantee, Salisbury telegraphed to Layard on May 24: the Anglo-Turkish Convention was accordingly signed in Constantinople on June 4. "Thus the policy which had been slowly formulated by Beaconsfield, Home, Layard and Salisbury was put into effect almost overnight."[47] The agreement which had been concluded with Austria completed Salisbury's network. Whatever trouble might be expected from the French, the successful conclusion of the Berlin conference, which rested largely on the satisfactory working of Salisbury's secret agreements, had to be considered first. In point of fact Lyons showed himself to be not very optimistic about the eventual reactions of Waddington; he even thought that if the French minister had a knowledge of the plan concerning Cyprus he would create difficulties about attending the Congress. If by prudence Salisbury left him in ignorance until the very end, the surprise would

[45] Newton, *op. cit.*, Vol. II, p. 139.
[46] S.P., France Drafts, 1878-80, Salisbury to Lyons, May 16 and 22, Private.
[47] Lee, *op. cit.*, p. 85.

doubtless be very disagreeable for the French; but on the other hand it might be better "to have got the congress well to work before running any risk of causing a secession, and it [might] be easier to deal with a protest made after, than one made before the event".[48] That was certainly the opinion of Salisbury himself; there was a risk to be taken but it was henceforward impossible to turn back: "I am sorry that your impressions of the mood in which the French are likely to receive the news when published are still so gloomy," he wrote on June 5 to Lyons. "However we must hope for the best . . . so I hope our friends at Paris will confine themselves to epigram." [49] At all events the Foreign Secretary felt confident that the use of the Tunisian bait at the right time would be enough to silence the possible scruples of the French delegation.

3. Bargaining at Berlin

All was ready for the Congress; the major decisions had been made beforehand, and in many cases the delegates would only have to ratify what had previously been agreed upon secretly. The Congress, however, was not to be a mere "farce". The very multiplicity of Salisbury's agreements exposed him to the danger of "technical incidents", as for instance the premature disclosure of the Anglo-Russian agreement (on June 14). In addition Salisbury had to cope with two unknown factors. The attitude of Italy was dubious,[50] and it was not clear what would be the French reaction to the Cyprus Convention. These uncertainties account for manifold secret dealings which it is often difficult to describe because some basic documents are still lacking, while the available testimonies are often biased and contradictory.[51]

It is very likely that at the beginning of the Congress the British and German negotiators agreed formally that a free hand in Tunis would be the French compensation for Russian, Austrian and British acquisitions; at all events it was only a confirmation of the contacts already taken in April and May. German agreement was perhaps given during the first meeting between Bismarck and Disraeli on June 11, 1878. It appears that Bismarck again suggested to Disraeli that he "take Egypt";

---

[48] S.P., France, 1878, Lyons to Salisbury, June 7, 1878.

[49] S.P., Paris Private Drafts, 1878–80, Salisbury to Lyons, June 5, 1878.

[50] In actual fact the Italian Government had instructed Corti to abide by the policy of "clean hands" and to refrain from seeking compensations, except if Austria should annex Bosnia-Herzegovina.

[51] This is specially the case with the Italian witnesses who laid stress alternately on the offers which were made to them, and on the virtuous conduct of the Italian delegation in the Berlin game of grab.

France would not be so vexed as might be imagined, and "in any case Tunis or Syria might be given her as an equivalent".[52] Bismarck obviously was still "in the dark" as to the Cyprus Convention. Disraeli did not correct his mistake and gave no answer to his suggestion; but it was out of the question for the British to seize Egypt. At all events Bismarck was soon informed of the agreement about Cyprus and warmly approved it. "You have done a wise thing," he said to Disraeli. "This is progress. It will be popular."[53]

Though Bismarck may have made the first direct offer of Tunis to the French delegates, it seems more plausible that Salisbury, as the author of the Cyprus Convention, brought forward the proposal which was to square France: in any case, Bismarck's suggestions about Tunis were not new, and his encouragements could not have the importance which Salisbury's subsequent promises were bound to have for the French. At the beginning of July the critical moment drew near for Salisbury. The Cyprus Convention depended upon Russia's retention of Kars, Ardahan or Batum; the discussion about the Asiatic territories took place on July 6. On the following night Lord Salisbury wrote a long personal letter to Waddington explaining the Convention and the circumstances which had made it necessary: Salisbury tried to sugar the pill by remarking that England had refused to take Egypt or Syria in consideration of French opposition, and added that Cyprus would be given back if the Russians abandoned their Asiatic conquests.[54] It was high time to inform the French, for on July 7 the *Daily Telegraph* gave the news of the Convention.

The French did not confine themselves "to epigram" as Salisbury had for some time hoped. While the Convention was giving rise to a burst of indignation in Paris, Waddington had an interview with Salisbury on July 7 and expressed his feelings. The time had come for Salisbury to make the sacrifices he had long been prepared for. In the course of a conversation which turned upon the whole Mediterranean problem, the British statesman told Waddington, "Do what you like there" (in Tunis), and during another interview, "You will be obliged

[52] Blowitz in *The Times*, April 5, 1881, quoting Bismarck himself. But the journalist thinks that it was only "one of the sallies he sometimes indulges in".

[53] Buckle, *op. cit.*, Vol. VI, p. 342. Buckle's assertion that "on the suggestion that France should have free scope in Tunis, [Disraeli] seems to have hesitated", is contradicted by the facts. The hesitations (if there were any) came before Berlin.

[54] D. E. Lee, *op. cit.*, p. 100; Newton, *op. cit.*, Vol. II, p. 149; Seton-Watson, *op. cit.*, p. 457.

to take it, you cannot leave Carthage in the hands of the barbarians."[55] A summary which Salisbury made some months later confirmed the general drift of his suggestions to Waddington, minus the flashes of style: "With respect to Tunis, I said that England was wholly disinterested and had no intention to contest the influence which the geographical position of Algeria naturally gave to France." If the Turkish Empire were to fall to pieces, Salisbury added, "as to Tunis . . . England would not hold herself bound to interfere with any course which France in such event might choose to take". [56] The presence of Disraeli at some of the interviews, and his approval of Salisbury's language as well as Bismarck's repeated assurances that Germany gave her total acquiescence in the proposal, gave more weight to declarations which were in themselves perfectly clear, even if (as Salisbury insisted later) allusions were made "to the rights and claims of other Powers, Turkey and Italy especially".[57] Waddington's first surprise (and perhaps hesitation)[58] passed off, the French plenipotentiaries decided to bring a motion before the Congress: but the French Government expressed its opposition to this step and the matter was temporarily shelved.[59] But Waddington was so obviously reassured by Salisbury's declarations that it was thereafter quite out of the question for him to show any opposition to, or even to express reserves about, the Anglo-Turkish Convention. Without any fixed ideas on the policy to be perfected in Tunisia (no direct and immediate annexation, but perhaps a protectorate with the occupation of strategic points), Waddington had already mentioned to Salisbury the possibility of some later action: "What we are determined to have", he told him, "is the formal recognition of the protectorate which we in fact exercise in this country, and to be entirely at liberty to extend our influence and to develop our interests as we see fit, without clashing with rival pretensions."

[55] Waddington's version was first given in his letter to d'Harcourt, July 21, 1878 (D.D.F., Vol. II, No. 330). In the despatch No. 332 (same date) Waddington resumes the same subject: "Prenez Tunis, si vous voulez, m'a dit Lord Salisbury; l'Angleterre ne s'y opposera pas et respectera vos décisions. D'ailleurs, a-t-il ajouté dans un autre entretien, vous ne pouvez pas laisser Carthage aux mains des Barbares." Salisbury tried later to accredit a version attenuating the vigour of his Berlin utterances but never denied the accuracy of Waddington's recollections.

[56] Cecil, op. cit., Vol. II, p. 332, Salisbury to Layard, October 1878.

[57] Newton, op. cit., Vol. II, p. 158, Salisbury to Lyons, July 24, 1878.

[58] According to Freycinet, Waddington refused to listen to "ces démons tentateurs". Cf. G. de Freycinet, Souvenirs (Paris, 1913), p. 34.

[59] G. Hanotaux, Histoire de la France contemporaine (Paris, 1903–8), Vol. IV, pp. 387 and 388.

If the French delegation appeared satisfied, there was still an Italian problem to solve. Strictly speaking the solution which had been given to the question of Bosnia-Herzegovina (the mere "occupation" by Austria) did not justify an Italian demand for compensations, but the Italian delegates could not but feel uneasy about the unexpected Cyprus Convention of which Corti learnt in the newspapers on July 7, and fear the reaction of Italian public opinion when they returned to Rome with clean but empty hands. It was probably to soothe this disappointment that Bülow, the second German plenipotentiary, after the publication of the Convention, told Corti: "L'Angleterre à Chypre, pourquoi ne prendriez vous pas Tunis en vous arrangeant avec l'Angleterre?" (July 8).[60] There is no evidence that Bismarck was informed of this offer (and Bülow perhaps did not know of the understanding between the Chancellor and Salisbury about Tunis): the Chancellor always asserted that he had played a straightforward game with France in Berlin, but Bismarck, while encouraging France to seize Tunis, obviously aimed, among other things, at creating friction with Italy,[61] and would have been perfectly capable of offering Tunis to the French and at the same time proposing it to Italy through Bülow, the more so as Waddington had at first received Salisbury's offer with reserve.[62] At all events Corti's answer was negative: "Vous voulez donc nous brouiller avec la France?"

British offers to the Italian plenipotentiaries are shrouded in the same mystery. According to Count de Launay, second Italian delegate, the question of the cession of Tripoli to Italy was ventilated during a conversation which he had with Salisbury: de Launay expressed his regret that Italy was not informed of the Cyprus Convention before its publication, and Salisbury, de Launay reported, "did his best to explain the circumstance, and allowed me to infer, from his veiled

[60] Chiali, op. cit., p. 91.

[61] P. Knaplund, Letters from the Berlin Embassy (Washington, 1944), p. 135.

[62] Holstein confirms the reality of the German (and Austrian) propositions to Italy ("The suggestion was put by Germany and Austria that Italy should annex Tunisia"), propositions "flatly rejected" by Corti: cf. N. Rich and M. H. Fisher, Holstein Papers, Vol. I (Cambridge, 1955), p. 105. On his side Corti was convinced that Bismarck was informed of Bülow's proposal. Cf. S. Gwynn and G. M. Tuckwell, The Life of Charles Dilke (London, 1917), Vol. I, p. 382. The French categorically denied that any offer had been made (Freycinet to Say, June 10, 1880, in D.D.F., Vol. III). Langer, op. cit., p. 71, remarks also that Bismarck only spoke to Waddington about Tunis on July 13, after Bülow's offer to Corti and Corti's refusal: but there had been a preliminary agreement between Salisbury and Bismarck about France and Tunis. It is difficult to reach a conclusion for want of satisfactory evidence.

utterances, that Italy might dream of expansion in the direction of Tripoli or Tunis. I was not authorized to enter upon a discussion on this point," de Launay concluded. The accuracy of de Launay's recollections about "Tunis" may be questioned, but it seems that "Tripoli" was actually mentioned by Salisbury in his conversations with Corti: "Lord Salisbury advised me to take Tripoli," Corti told Dilke later.[63] There is at least some evidence that in the course of the discussions about Tunis, Waddington mentioned the possible opposition of Italy and that Salisbury suggested "that Italy might seek compensation in Tripoli".[64] The fact of the suggestions seems indisputable; it is more difficult to reach a conclusion about their exact significance. It can be imagined that Salisbury, not particularly keen to arbitrate in a Franco-Italian conflict over Tunisia, and whose sympathies were undoubtedly on the side of France, was at this time primarily concerned to have the occupation of Cyprus accepted by all the other Powers. It is therefore probable that, without informing the Italians of the suggestions which he had made to Waddington (he did not speak about it except on August 13, 1878, to Menabrea, adding that he had met with little enthusiasm from his interlocutor), Salisbury spoke about compensations for Italy and evoked prospects of African expansion. But he deliberately expressed himself in rather vague terms, so that the Italian diplomats could have thought that he was indicating Tunis and Tripoli equally as objects of their ambitions. One cannot but concur with Dilke's conclusion that "the labours of the Berlin Congress, or its festivities so confused the minds of the plenipotentiaries, that they have never been clear who offered what to whom; but it at least seems plain ... that a great deal of offering of other people's property took place".[65]

The free hand given to France in Tunis by Salisbury was only one of the acts of "international brigandage"[66] perpetrated in Berlin, others being the deal about Cyprus and the occupation of Bosnia-Herzegovina. In the three cases the European diplomats had done what Salisbury

[63] Gwynn and Tuckwell, *op. cit.*, Vol. I, p. 382. But Corti in May 1881 emphatically denied that such a conversation had ever taken place "either at Berlin or elsewhere" (Crispi, *op. cit.*, Vol. II, p. 114 and Public Record Office, Granville Papers (G.P.) 30/29/182). Dilke, however, was very sceptical about a denial which was intended to clear Italy of any participation in the Berlin bargainings at a time when France had just seized Tunis in consequence of Berlin proposals.

[64] G.P. 30/29/143, Lyons to Salisbury, July 19, 1878.

[65] Sir Charles Dilke, *The Present Position of European Politics* (London, 1887), p. 27.

[66] Newton, *op. cit.*, Vol. II, p. 105.

was afterwards to try to acquit himself of doing, and had "given away other people's property without their consent".[67] Several considerations, however, made the Tunisian bargain less defensible than the other Berlin arrangements. While in the case of Cyprus and Bosnia the Porte had given its consent (not without strong pressure), it had never been contemplated that there should be any kind of regard for its rights of suzerainty in Tunis. The Regency, too, was not a mere Ottoman province liable to be separated from the Porte in expiation of Turkish errors, but a wholly autonomous principality. A totally Moslem country, Tunis presented none of the national and religious problems which could in other regions of the Ottoman Empire serve as a pretext or an excuse for annexation by the Powers. Lastly, the case of Tunis was unique owing to the fact that there was a well-established British policy there which had tended precisely to prevent France from seizing the country, a policy which had been completely reversed in Berlin.

That startling but calculated change in British policy towards Tunis originated in motives which, as we have already remarked, largely went outside the limits of Tunisian problems: the Regency had only appeared in Berlin as "small change" which was used to balance the transactions made by the Powers. As had constantly happened since 1830, the major demands of British policy in Europe, and her relations with France and Turkey, had taken precedence over Britain's traditional attitude in Tunis.

The search for responsibilities is fruitless. There is no doubt that Bismarck had taken the initiative in the matter and undertaken to tempt the Foreign Office with gilded prospects of compensation. But it is none the less obvious that Salisbury had eagerly availed himself of the offer when it had been clear that for the realization of his plans for the settlement of the Eastern crisis Tunis could be used as a suitable compensation for France. Lord Newton's thesis that it is unjustifiable to make Lord Salisbury responsible for the Tunis affair on the ground that "all that he had done was to intimate that he had heard that the French were extremely anxious to go to Tunis, that if they did so British interests would not be endangered",[68] is indefensible: Bismarck was perhaps "the real instigator of the Tunis expedition", but for the French Government it was the British authorization which really mattered since Britain, not Germany, had successfully stopped their advance in the Regency since 1830.

[67] Cecil, *op. cit.*, Vol. II, p. 333.
[68] Newton, *op. cit.*, Vol. II, pp. 250 and 251.

Salisbury probably thought, first, that this was the price of European Peace—this had been Bismarck's thesis from the beginning and his programme had been finally adopted by the Powers—secondly that as in any case Tunis seemed destined soon to fall into the hands of some European Power it was to Britain's interest to reap as much practical profit as possible from the inevitable destruction of Tunisian independence. But experience was to show elsewhere (in Persia and China for instance) that such a result was in no way inevitable and that the rivalry of the Powers could give rise to some kind of equilibrium through which the independence of the country concerned was preserved, with difficulty but lastingly. By destroying that equilibrium in Tunis Salisbury threw the Regency into a peril which was to lead fatally to its political annihilation.

4. Salisbury and the Berlin Engagements

The Berlin engagements were the less ambiguous in that they corresponded to a change in British policy and met precise diplomatic necessities, and were the outcome of very clear discussions with Germany. Nevertheless, when the time came to confirm them and to put them on record, the Foreign Office became unexpectedly reticent.

The reactions to the Cyprus agreement had been very hostile in Paris: "furious cries were raised . . . that England was threatening French influence in the Mediterranean as well as in Egypt", and some newspapers had advocated the rejection of the convention by the French delegation at Berlin.[69] The French Government were afraid of the opposition of the Chambers and somewhat divided on the question of Tunis on account of the difficulties which were likely to arise with Italy.[70] Once in Paris Waddington considered that the only way of defending his policy was to act immediately upon Salisbury's promises and to bind the Foreign Office by an engagement more official than the informal conversations of Berlin.[71]

Waddington overcame the hesitations of his colleagues and persuaded

[69] Sir Sidney Lee, King Edward VII (London, 1925), Vol. I, p. 366, and E. Malcolm Carroll, French Public Opinion and Foreign Affairs (New York, 1931), p. 77. See also Lyons' letters to Salisbury, July 9, 12 and 16, 1878, in S.P., France, 1878.

[70] According to Hanotaux (Vol. IV, p. 388) President MacMahon was particularly violent, "Ils veulent nous f... l'Italie sur le dos, maintenant... Jamais je ne consentirai; je ne veux pas qu'on nous jette dans une nouvelle querelle."

[71] "Il serait fort possible que dans trois mois d'ici les Anglais aient changé d'avis", Waddington wrote to d'Harcourt on July 21 (D.D.F., Vol. II).

them to take advantage of the *carte blanche* given in Berlin. On July 19 he wrote to Roustan that France could "être amenée sous peu à affirmer son protectorat sur la Régence de Tunis", and that Roustan could consider "le consentement de l'Angleterre et de l'Allemagne comme acquis" but that "il fallait tenir compte du mécontentement de l'Italie".[72] At the same time Waddington met Lord Lyons on the 18th, and informed him of assurances given by Salisbury and Beaconsfield that H.M. Government would make "no objection whatever" if it suited France to take possession of the Regency of Tunis and of Salisbury's suggestion that Italy might seek compensation in Tripoli. France, Waddington went on, did not intend to take "absolute possession of Tunis" but could exercise "a preponderant and exclusive influence there": for the time being, in order to reconcile public opinion, Waddington was anxious to be able "to produce these explanations and assurances in a written, official and so to speak binding shape".[73]

Waddington's straightforward request placed the British Government in an embarrassing situation. On the one hand it was difficult to receive French overtures with coldness: the promises made in Berlin were undeniable, and Salisbury probably did not regret them. But on the other hand, as the Cyprus Convention had met with serious criticism from the Opposition and from some elements of public opinion, it was likely that the disclosure of the Tunis agreement would have given rise to a storm of protests. Salisbury was also too well aware of Italian dissatisfaction with the Berlin Treaty to face the irritation which was likely to arise in Italy, not to mention the reactions of the Porte. Salisbury's answer to Lyons on July 20 reflected these difficulties: the British Government wished to answer Waddington's demand in a way calculated to maintain their good relations with France and to make his own personal task easier. As for the subject of his interview with Lyons, however, it was difficult to make it the subject of binding assurances because the contingencies under which these assurances would receive a practical application were difficult to foresee. If France occupied Tunis tomorrow "we should not even remonstrate", Salisbury continued, "but to promise that publicly would be a little difficult", as Great Britain could not give away "other people's property" nor overlook probable Italian objections. In these circumstances Salisbury suggested that Waddington in his despatch "should avoid putting categorical questions which we would not be able to answer precisely as he wishes", but should make a statement in general terms of the

[72] D.D.F., Vol. II, Waddington to Roustan, July 19, 1878.
[73] G.P. 30/29/143, Lyons to Salisbury, July 19, 1878.

points of the African Coast in which France took an interest, "leaving us to make such assurances as we think we can properly give".[74]

Lord Lyons immediately had an interview with Waddington, and informed him of Lord Salisbury's intentions. "I particularly urged upon him the importance of not making [his communication] peremptory or too definite and categorical, but on the contrary of giving you the opportunity to offer him friendly assurances, rather than demanding them." The French minister assured Lord Lyons that this was indeed his aim.[75] But Waddington's first letter to d'Harcourt was in effect far from meeting Salisbury's requirements: it was full of blunt references to "the barbarians", and asked for the formal assent ("leur consentement formel... une réponse catégorique") of the British "à tout ce qu'il nous conviendrait de faire à Tunis *y compris l'annexion*"—in short, for a *carte blanche* in Tunis. This vigorous terminology caused a flutter in London: Waddington had given rein to his "dramatic instinct",[76] and although the general tenor of his recollections was quite accurate "his vivacious French" by no means rendered the tone of Salisbury's communications and, what was of more importance, overlooked the rights and claims of other Powers, Turkey and Italy especially. "He makes me talk of Tunis and Carthage as if they had been my own personal property and I was making him a liberal wedding present. . . . What I told him," Salisbury concluded, "was, that if a state of things should arise in which there was no other obstacle to his occupying Tunis but our objection, that objection would not be made." Salisbury then again suggested that Waddington should put his quotations in a more diplomatic form.[77] Lyons busied himself once more in Paris with trying to convince Waddington that he should rewrite the despatch which had incurred this criticism. The minister showed little willingness, perhaps, judged Lyons, because he did not want to appear in the eyes of his own Department to have withdrawn the despatch; and he suggested sending instructions to d'Harcourt to give Lord Salisbury the assurance that the despatch would not be published.[78] In the end, Waddington, while still insisting on his version of the Berlin conversations ("Je tenais... à reproduire avec une

[74] S.P., Paris Drafts, 1878–80.

[75] S.P., France, 1878, Lyons to Salisbury, July 21.

[76] *Letters of Queen Victoria*, Vol. II, Salisbury to Queen Victoria, July 25, 1878.

[77] Newton, *op. cit.*, Vol. II, pp. 158 and 159. Salisbury to Lyons, July 24, 1878, private. The "official despatch" (F.O. 27/2300, July 24) is even more prudent and Salisbury therein carries out the *tour de force* of not using the word "Tunis" although constantly speaking of it.

[78] S.P., France, 1878, Lyons to Salisbury, July 26, 1878.

fidélité absolue le langage du Ministre anglais"), sent to London an "attenuated" account of the conversations which could easily get by under the eyes of the Cabinet.

During conversations on the Mediterranean situation, he wrote to d'Harcourt, the attention of the two ministers had been drawn to Tunisia:

"Lord Salisbury n'ignorait pas la sollicitude que devait causer au gouvernement français le sort de ce petit pays, dont la situation intérieure est si précaire et sur lequel son voisinage immédiat avec l'Algérie nous oblige à tenir constamment l'œil ouvert. Allant de lui même au devant des préoccupations qu'il pouvait nous supposer, il s'est appliqué à me faire entendre, dans le langage le plus amical et le plus explicite à la fois, que l'Angleterre était décidée à ne nous susciter aucun obstacle de ce côté, que, dans sa pensée, il ne devait tenir qu'à nous seuls de régler au gré de nos convenances la nature et l'étendue de nos rapports avec le Bey, et que le gouvernement de la Reine acceptait d'avance toutes les conséquences que pourrait impliquer, pour la destination ultérieure du territoire tunisien, le développement naturel de notre politique. 'Faites à Tunis ce que vous jugerez convenable, m'a dit Sa Seigneurie, l'Angleterre ne s'y opposera pas et respectera vos décisions'. Revenant dans une autre occasion sur ce sujet, Lord Salisbury n'hésitait pas à me confier qu'il regardait comme moralement impossible que le régime actuel pût durer à Tunis et qu'aux yeux du Cabinet anglais il appartenait à la France de présider à la régénération de ce pays consacré par de grands souvenirs."[79]

The tenor of Salisbury's despatch of August 7 was discussed in the Cabinet: it gave a final statement of the significance of British engagements towards France, and although "secret" it was meant for the British and French archives. "We feel that, however carefully it is worded," Salisbury commented to Lyons, "it may make mischief between us and Italy, if published in a defiant manner by the French." Here again, Salisbury made certain reservations concerning the expressions which had been attributed to him—reservations which were designed to attenuate the meaning of his promises. The Berlin con-

[79] D.D.F., Vol. II, Waddington to d'Harcourt, July 25 and 26, 1878. It is perhaps the memory of this difficult haggling which, a few weeks later, led Disraeli to express the following unflattering appreciation of Waddington: "I think Waddington, tho' he may not always intend it, a somewhat dangerous animal to deal with" (S.P., Beaconsfield to Salisbury, September 3, 1878).

versations, he pointed out, had been of a private nature, and so Salisbury had not taken any notes:

> "I am consequently unable to affirm that M. Waddington has reproduced the precise words made use of then either by himself or me. I am rather disposed to think that, though he has used the form of quotation, he merely desired to indicate the general bearing of our communications, and especially the amicable feelings towards France by which my language was inspired. So far, and without being able to confirm the exact phrases attributed to me, I have great pleasure in bearing witness to the general justice of his recollections."

As for the actual contents of the discussions, the despatch of August 7 put in strong terms restrictions which had underlain his previous communications with Waddington. The British Government had witnessed "with lively satisfaction the success of the experiment conducted by France in Algeria": her presence on those shores, "supported as it [was] by an imposing military force", gave her "the power of pressing with decisive force upon the Government of the neighbouring province of Tunis". This was a result which the British Government had "long recognized as inevitable and . . . accepted without reluctance. England [had] no special interests in this region which could possibly lead her to view with apprehension or distrust the legitimate and expanding influence of France." Salisbury, however, had not "foreboded an early fall of the existing government of Tunis" and his information rather led him to expect that if it was disturbed by no external shock it might "last for a considerable time". Lastly, Salisbury had drawn Waddington's attention to the interest which Italy took in the Tunisian question: as no communication had been made with the Italian Government on this matter, the British Government had not arrived "at any opinion upon the position which Italy [might] take up in reference to the region under discussion".[80] Salisbury had come very far indeed from the "barbarians" and his despatch contained no more than a promise of neutrality, with some thorns attached.

From his tone and arguments, it was clear that the Foreign Office wished for nothing so much as a lull in Tunis which would defer the moment when France would avail herself of the *carte blanche* which she had been given. This result could be achieved through the Italian opposition which the conclusion of the despatch of August 7 foreshadowed.

[80] State Papers, Vol. XCIX (1881), *Affairs of Tunis*, I, Salisbury to Lyons, August 7, 1878.

News about the Tunis agreement had begun to leak out immediately after the conclusion of the Congress,[81] and had reached Tunis and Italy before the end of July. Wood was of course deeply disturbed by these rumours, and as early as July 23, 1878, asked for authorization to give them a formal denial "in order to remove the impression which [they were] calculated to produce upon the mind of His Highness as well as of the population".[82] Salisbury gave an answer which, in the light of the prudent despatch which he had sent to Lyons on the same day, was not altogether inaccurate but was at least misleading: "no offer of the annexation of Tunis to France has ever been made by Her Majesty's Government to the French Government", he wrote on August 7.[83] Wood was left in complete ignorance of what had really happened in Berlin; Salisbury's laconic answer, however, did not lend itself to a lengthy treatment, and Wood had to use Disraeli's speech of July 18, 1878, in the Lords, and his references to the preservation of Turkish territorial integrity in support of British traditional policy in Tunis. The lack of indications received from the Foreign Office thus allowed Wood to continue a dangerous struggle against French policy in Tunis.

In Italy, the uneasiness which was felt about Tunis was added to the disappointment and irritation of public opinion after the Berlin settlement. In August General Menabrea, the Italian Ambassador, attacked the question of Tunis with Salisbury. The answer was again wholly ambiguous: Salisbury did not think it "likely" that France should want to interfere with the existing government of Tunis, but at the same time he indicated that, apart from the problem of freedom of trade, "the question of the occupation of Tunis by France was not a question of a character to cause serious anxiety to Her Majesty's government".[84] The Italians would have been wise to take into consideration the veiled warning which was included in Salisbury's words; but nearly at the same time Macdonell gave in Rome a much more categorical denial to the rumours about Tunis. "Whatever the French Government may think," Macdonell told Corti, "[Corti] certainly would not for a moment suppose that Her Majesty's Government could offer to dispose of that which was not theirs to dispose of."[85] It was enough to reassure

---

[81] La Liberté (Paris) and Montagsblatt (Vienna) had printed it on July 16.
[82] F.O. 102/111, Wood to Salisbury, July 23, 1878.
[83] M. Safwat, Tunis and the Great Powers (Alexandria, 1943), p. 236; F.O. 102/111, Salisbury to Wood, August 7, 1878.
[84] F.O. 45/334, Salisbury to Macdonell, August 21, 1878.
[85] F.O. 45/340, Macdonell to Salisbury, August 26, 1878.

the Italian Government and encourage them to continue an active policy in Tunis which was to bring them in opposition with France. In August Mussi, on special mission in Tunis, proposed to the Tunisian Government an agreement with Italy about Bizerta, and in September opposed the renewal by the Bey of de Sancy's agricultural concession, at the risk, as we shall see later, of provoking a Franco-Tunisian incident. For this situation, Salisbury's not altogether straightforward game was partly responsible.

Waddington was fully aware of the obstacles which stood in the way of France in Tunis, and especially of the Italian problem which Salisbury had raised in his despatch of August 7. While announcing a plan for a Treaty of protectorate to Lyons, Waddington tried to sound the Ambassador about Italy and suggested the possibility of conciliating her by the offer of Tripoli. Although Lyons remained reserved and suggested rather a policy of waiting in Tunis in order to avoid any *action d'éclat* which would arouse Italy's hostility, Waddington stuck to his idea: "There was something very attractive in the idea of introducing civilization into the countries of the South and East of the Mediterranean," he told Lyons. ". . . As a means to this end might be regarded the occupation of Tunis by France and of Tripoli by Italy, the joint action of France and England in Egypt, and the position taken up by England with regard to Asia Minor." [86] At the beginning of September, in the course of two interviews with Salisbury (September 2 in Dieppe and September 4 in Paris), Waddington took up the question again. But Salisbury was no more encouraging than Lyons, and declined to give any kind of encouragement to the idea of obtaining from Turkey the cession of Tripoli to Italy. It was certainly largely because of that lack of support in London that on September 5 Waddington informed Roustan that the affair of the protectorate was to "subir un temps d'arrêt qui pourra être long".[87] Several reasons were given for the postponement of the project (the problem of compensation for Italy and the necessity of neutralizing Wood's action) but they had the same British source and originated in Salisbury's subtle but systematic " revisionism" which was actually obstructing French action in Tunis.

On the other hand, Salisbury renewed his indirect warnings to Italy nearly verbatim at the beginning of October in order to incite her to prudence. Any unconsidered Italian action was likely to provoke an immediate and perhaps decisive French riposte, and thereby break the

[86] F.O. 27/2312, Lyons to Salisbury, August 17, 1878.
[87] D.D.F., Vol. II, Waddington to Roustan, September 5.

S.A.P.—I

fragile equilibrium which he was trying to maintain in Tunis. "A war between France and Italy," Salisbury wrote to Wood in September, "would almost certainly result from the acquisition of territory or special privileges in Tunis" by Italy.[88] At the same time Salisbury reacted to Waddington's complaints about Wood's aggressive language and attitude, by urging prudence on the Bey, thus completing the arrangements he had made to avert an explosion of the Tunisian question: it was the Bey's interest to live at peace with France and Italy and "to avoid giving to either Power any legitimate cause of complaint. If such a policy [was] carefully observed ... there [was] no reason to anticipate that neighbouring Powers [would] form any wishes inconsistent with his security."[89] Salisbury undoubtedly expected that Wood would read between the lines and turn this advice to the best account for his own conduct. But Wood was perfectly able to ignore such hints when they ran counter to what he considered to be British interests.

5. Salisbury Gives more Pledges to France

The double thrust of Italy and France, and the de Sancy affair, were soon to break the lull which Salisbury had hoped to prolong by his prudent attitude and the restraint he had tried to put on the competition of both Powers for preponderance in Tunis. The crisis ultimately led him to give France more substantial pledges than he had perhaps first expected to do.

In spite of Salisbury's and Waddington's warnings, Italy definitely adopted an active policy in Tunis, especially after the constitution of the Depretis ministry in December 1878. Maccio's appointment as Agent in Tunis (that "very energetic" Consul had been on bad terms with Roustan when his colleague in Cairo and in Syria) and his spectacular installation in his new post (40 sailors of the despatch boat *Rapido* presented arms at the Consulate)[90] showed that Italy was resolved not to tolerate the seizure of Tunis by any other Power and to continue the struggle for predominance in Tunis, a policy which the French Government thought to be unacceptable and precluded by the Berlin agreements.

At the same time the outbreak of the de Sancy affair was interpreted in Paris as the first outcome of Italian intrigues, locally supported by

[88] F.O. 102/111, Salisbury to Wood, September 18, 1878.
[89] F.O. 102/111, Salisbury to Wood, October 19, 1878.
[90] F.O. 102/111, Wood to Salisbury, October 8, 1878 and December 31, 1878. For a detailed account of Maccio's career see J. Ganiage, *op. cit.*, pp. 550–4.

Wood. De Sancy, a French gentleman, had obtained in 1866 the concession of 3,000 acres of land for the purpose of breeding a specified number of horses and cattle; the concession had been afterwards extended to 12,000 acres.[91] It had, however, appeared in 1878 that de Sancy had not the number of animals provided for by the contract and the Bey had decided to cancel the concession, with the assent of the Commission of Control which had been created *ad hoc* and which comprised a Tunisian official, the Austrian Consul and Queillé, the French Inspecteur Général (of the International Commission of the Debt). The matter came to a crisis when Roustan intervened and opposed the commission's entering the Sidi Tabet estate on the pretext that it was a "terre française" (December 1878). There is no doubt that the Bey was within his rights: the attitude of Queillé, which was deemed "strange" in Paris,[92] is quite clear in this respect and Roustan himself admitted that the Bey might be "strictly in the right", but he made the matter one of prestige for his government and laid claim to privileges of jurisdiction for French enterprises in Tunis such as were not likely to be accepted by the Bey. But while in the similar conflict which had arisen between the Bey and Italy about the Djedeida estate (1871) Great Britain had co-operated with France to limit Italian demands, this time the Foreign Office retired from the field.

The French Government took precautionary measures: as they were to do at each important stage of the Tunisian question they first turned to Bismarck with an account of the de Sancy affair, Italian intrigues and Wood's alleged hostility, and asked for fresh assurances of support. The answer was as satisfactory as it could be: "Je crois que la poire tunisienne est mûre et qu'il est temps pour vous de la cueillir," Bismarck told Saint Vallier. Bismarck also informed the French Ambassador that he had warned the Italians that "à [ses] yeux Tunis [était] compris dans l'orbite français",[93] and that Andrassy had disavowed the action of the Austrian Consul. What was still better, the Chancellor had entered into communication about Tunis with Disraeli whose "largeur de vues" he had appreciated in Berlin and not with Salisbury "ce *clergyman* laïque obstiné et maladroit". In actual fact, Bülow had been instructed on January 3 to see Lord Odo Russell about Tunis "et lui demander s'il peut être vrai que le Consul Anglais...

---

[91] J. Ganiage, *op. cit.*, pp. 533–8, deals comprehensively with this intricate affair.

[92] F.O. 27/2318, Lyons to Salisbury, December 29, 1878: Queillé was immediately recalled to Paris and explanations were asked from him about his "ranging [himself] in opposition to the flag of his country".

[93] D.D.F., Vol. II, Saint Vallier to Waddington, January 5, 1879.

ait joué un rôle inamical envers la France.... Nous avions pensé,"
Bismarck added, "que la politique anglaise ne devait pas sentir le besoin
de gêner la France à Tunis". The Chancellor wished that "les agisse-
ments de M. Wood" should not endanger friendly relations between
France and Britain, and he concluded that he had made up his mind to
lend the moral support of Germany to Mr Waddington in his Tunisian
policy whatever it would be.[94]

Salisbury answered that Wood "s'était tenu en dehors de l'incident
actuel et qu'il [n'avait] donné à la France... aucun sujet de mécontentement".[95] But, possibly as a result of Bismarck's suggestions, formal
instructions were sent at the same time to Wood which fully met
Bismarck's requirements. "You should maintain an attitude of strict
neutrality on this question," wrote Salisbury to Wood on January 8,
"and should not interfere in any way."[96] The Foreign Office had
already intimated to the Italian Government that the alleged French
intention to assume the protectorate of Tunis was not a matter "that
directly [touched] any interest of England" and that therefore it was
not likely that Great Britain would interfere.[97] With Great Britain
adopting this position, the Bey could not expect to stand French pressure any more: an ultimatum having been presented by Roustan
(January 7, 1879) the Bey turned for the last time to Wood and asked
him if he would formally guarantee Tunisian territory in case the
Tunisian Government should refuse to accept part of the French
demands. Wood could not but answer that he had no authority to
give any such guarantee. The Bey then yielded to the French demands
regarding the confirmation of the de Sancy concession, public apolo-
gies and dismissal of some Tunisian officials made responsible for the
difficulty.

French policy had triumphed:[98] the moderating influence of the
International Commission was definitely eliminated by Queillé's recall

[94] P.E.A., Vol. III, Herbert von Bismarck to Bülow, January 3, 1879.

[95] D.D.F., Vol. II, Saint Vallier to Waddington, January 9, 1879. See also S.P.,
Paris Drafts, 1878–80, Salisbury to Lyons, January 4, 1879.

[96] F.O. 102/124, Salisbury to Wood, January 8, 1879.

[97] F.O. 45/375, Salisbury to Paget, January 6, 1879.

[98] Although the hopes nourished in Paris had been disappointed in the end,
since by submitting to the ultimatum presented by Roustan, the Bey prevented
the departure of the expedition which had been kept ready at Toulon. Taken by
surprise at the capitulation of the Tunisians, Waddington had not thought of
including in his ultimatum any guarantee for the future: the success of January
1879 did not have any repercussions and the question of a protectorate, taken up
again too late, dragged on inconclusively (J. Ganiage, op. cit., pp. 543–7).

and the nomination of Financial Inspectors more devoted to French political interests in Tunis. Roustan expressed the hope that the Bey would henceforth consult him more frequently on subjects relating to the foreign policy of the Regency and that he would "consider him as a Tunisian Functionary". The proposal, Wood remarked, indicated that France was now trying to establish a moral protectorate over the Regency.[99] For his own part Wood came off discredited from the crisis: there can be little doubt that he had (with Maccio's support) induced the Bey to resist French pressure; it was not to be expected that Wood could abstain altogether from the struggle for influence which was going on, and to which he had devoted his life in Syria as well as in Tunis. But at the decisive moment, Wood had failed to receive the backing of his government. The time had come for the French to remove the obstacle which his presence still constituted for their policy in Tunis.

Waddington, strengthened by Bismarck's support, renewed the offensive against Wood which he had started as early as September 1878, when he had suggested to Lord Salisbury that he should recall him from Tunis. Wood, he told Lyons, was at the bottom of the de Sancy affair and had instigated the Bey to resist French demands; his presence in Tunis "immensely increased" French difficulties.[100] Without going so far as to make an official request for Wood's recall, the French minister, in a private letter to his British colleague, reminded him of the half-promise made a few months earlier and concluded that the moment had perhaps come "to put into execution the measure you considered necessary then".[101]

It is difficult to say whether, as Bismarck seemed to think, Salisbury was really less inclined than Disraeli to satisfy French demands; such an attitude would have been pretty well in keeping with his "post-Berlin" policy. Certainly there is no document to indicate that Salisbury had ever encouraged the Consul's initiatives, although he had left him somewhat in the dark about the new British policy in Tunis. Wood however did not need encouragement to pursue a policy which was now meaningless—since Great Britain had abandoned her political objectives and accepted French predominance—and dangerous—since,

[99] F.O. 102/124, Wood to Salisbury, January 16, 1879.
[100] F.O. 27/2361, Lyons to Salisbury, January 10, 1879.
[101] S.P., France, 1879–80, Waddington to Salisbury, January 13, 1879. According to Waddington Lord Salisbury had then admitted "that Mr Wood was too old an offender to mend his ways, and that there was nothing to be done but to recall him".

as had clearly appeared during the de Sancy affair, the Foreign Office was not ready to fulfil the hopes to which Wood's activity could give rise in Tunis and Rome. Wood's presence in Tunis was bound to embroil the situation, and involve Britain in serious difficulties with France. "I should be very sorry to do anything disagreeable to the French with regard to Tunis," Lyons remarked on January 14, and this opinion was shared in London by many people who thought that the Berlin engagements precluded any kind of action hostile to France in Tunis.[102] Moreover, the Foreign Office could not fail to take Bismarck's warning and advice into consideration. Wood's recall was accordingly decided on in the beginning of 1879, and Salisbury authorized Lyons to inform the Quai d'Orsay unofficially that London had found a means to relieve Wood of his post in Tunis in the very near future.

As "a general massacre of aged official innocents" was contemplated shortly by the Foreign Office, it was hoped that the departure of Wood, who was beyond the age limit, would take place quickly and without creating the impression of an abrupt change of policy on the part of Great Britain, or of a concession to the pressure exerted by Paris. "I think that on the whole his absence will conduce to the good relations between the two countries, for he had lived too long in one atmosphere and was too much wedded to a policy which has ceased to have any meaning": such was Salisbury's funeral oration, in the letter in which he announced to Waddington the elegant solution thus provided for the problem of Wood.[103] But the hopes of the Foreign Office were disappointed and the Consul had a very narrow escape from the age limit (70 years), probably at the price of a slight twisting of the truth: Wood who was 73 claimed to be 67—'he entered the service 55 years ago, and therefore must have begun his public labours at a precocious age", Salisbury incredulously commented. The Foreign Office was thus somewhat at a loss to explain so sudden a dismissal (it was to take effect on April 1, 1879). Ultimately a "somewhat ignominious compromise" was resorted to: under the pretext of a reorganization of the consular service in the East the Consulate of Tunis was to be placed on a reduced footing, the establishment being "on a larger scale than present circumstances appear to require" (the Consul's salary was to be reduced from £1,600 to £900). In these conditions the Foreign Office was obliged to deprive itself of Wood's "valuable services". "I am happy to assure you," Salisbury wrote to Wood on February 26,

[102] Newton, *op. cit.*, Vol. II, p. 165, Lyons to Salisbury, January 14, 1879.
[103] S.P., Paris Drafts, 1878–80, Salisbury to Waddington, January 22, 1879.

"that the zeal and ability which you have shown in the discharge of your duties are highly appreciated by Her Majesty's Government." It is useless to dwell on Wood's distress when he was informed of Salisbury's decision. Emotion was universal in Tunis, where it was felt that, with Wood's removal, a fifty-year-old policy was coming to an abrupt end. Great Britain was officially withdrawing from Tunis and abandoning the Regency to Franco-Italian rivalry. As Salisbury wrote to Lyons, after having informed him of Wood's removal: "I think the French will find difficulties enough with Italy if they ever try to increase their influence in Tunis; but that is no affair of ours. We have hot water enough elsewhere without desiring to boil any in Tunis."[104]

Salisbury's expectations about Italy's resistance to French policy in Tunis were not mistaken: Italy had not lost hope and Depretis (and Cairoli after June 1879) tried to cultivate British friendship in order to get British support in Tunis. But the efforts of the Italians to drive a wedge between Britain and France and to arouse anxiety in London about French designs in Tunis were utterly unsuccessful. On no occasion did Salisbury depart from the attitude of neutrality which he had defined in 1878 in regard to an eventual French action in Tunis, or leave the least hope of Anglo-Italian co-operation in Tunis. This was already quite clear in January 1879 when, in spite of Italian hints, Salisbury refused to make any declaration in favour of the maintenance of the *status quo* in the Regency. Later on successive Italian overtures were all ignored by the Foreign Office. In March 1879, when Dupienne, a mere *Inspecteur des Domaines*, was appointed as Queillé's successor, Menabrea suggested some common action to remind the French Government that the agreement of 1869 provided for the independence of the French Inspectors: Salisbury let the matter drop until June and then contented himself with a mild and isolated observation in Paris.[105] In May 1879 an offer of discussion for an agreement about Mediterranean questions was likewise accepted for Salonica and Egypt, but refused with regard to Tunis. Lastly, in July 1879, the Italian Government proposed that in view of the difficult financial situation in Tunis the three Powers should consult and take action in common for the establishment of a Tunisian budget; although Stevens, the acting Consul General, seemed to approve Menabrea's suggestion, and although the

<hr>

[104] F.O. 102/125, Salisbury to Wood, February 24 and 26, 1879; Newton, *op. cit.*, Vol. II, p. 174, Salisbury to Lyons, March 6, 1879.

[105] F.O. 45/395, Menabrea to Salisbury, March 17, 1879; Salisbury to Lyons, June 3, 1879.

permanent officials of the Foreign Office thought it desirable that Great
Britain should join in a common action "if only to prevent the French
and Italians from coming to open antagonism", Salisbury's answer was
again negative. After having expressed his platonic regret about "the
disorder into which the affairs of the Regency were apparently falling",
Salisbury remarked that international budgets had not "as yet had a
brilliant success in Egypt" and concluded: "I think we had better
avoid, as long as we can, attempting a similar task for Tunis, in which
we really have no interest" (August 26, 1879).[106]

These successive failures to awake some interest in the Tunisian
question in Great Britain created at last an understandable discourage-
ment in Italy. "Nelle questioni dell'Egitto e di Tunisi," Count Maffei
remarked in July 1879, "il governo inglese non fa nulla per noi...
la buona intelligenza dell' Inghilterra... non esiste che nella immagina-
zione de Menebrea."[107] And Menabrea himself could not entertain
many illusions after the answer which Salisbury gave in December
1879 to a fresh offer of co-operation in Tunis. "In the case of Tunis,
where our interests are but indirect, I thought Her Majesty's Government should confine their action within limits as narrow as possible."[108]
It was clear that Salisbury was leaving the Regency to its fate, that is
to France with whom Great Britain had just concluded an agreement
about Egypt (September 1879). It seemed that the British Government, at the beginning of 1880, had abandoned the policy which Salisbury had sketched in 1878 and which aimed at delaying as far as possible
an eventual French action in the Regency. Germany being more
favourable than ever, Italy hostile but isolated, and Turkey impotent—
Salisbury had warned the Porte in July 1879 that it would do well
not to interfere in Tunis as it would "only do [itself] injury by provoking the hostility of France and thus bringing about a coalition
between that Power and Russia"[109]—the diplomatic circumstances
were very favourable to France, and it is probable that only the
threatening nature of international politics in 1879 had prevented her
from making a new attempt in Tunis. For Salisbury, the "Tunisian
question" was henceforward a closed book in the Franco-British
relations. Only a political incident at home, the success of the Liberals
in the 1880 election, was to revive the problem and pose once more the

[106] F.O. 45/396, Salisbury to Menabrea, August 9, 1879; F.O. 102/124, Note
by Salisbury, August 26, 1879.

[107] Giaccardi, op. cit., pp. 161-2, Maffei to Cairoli, July 19, 1879.

[108] F.O. 45/376, Salisbury to Paget, December 19, 1879.

[109] F.O. 78/2939, Salisbury to Layard, July 21, 1879.

question of the attitude of Great Britain with regard to French policy in Tunis.

If we would come to any conclusion about Salisbury's policy we should avoid both an apologia (which would take into consideration only the "interests" of Great Britain), and a judgement based exclusively on moral values. Let us try to look at the matter from inside Salisbury's system, and examine his Tunisian policy from the double point of view of the diplomatic technique it displays and of its results in the framework of British policy.

The diplomatic technique of Salisbury, in so far as it is revealed by the Tunisian question, is undeniably remarkable: one is constantly struck by his unerring vision, by the precision of his analyses, and by his ability to pick out the essential objects of British policy and subordinate to them all secondary considerations. In carrying out this clearly defined policy, there are neither hesitation nor regrets. Equally impressive is the really masterly "style" of Salisbury as Foreign Secretary. There enters into Salisbury's policy a "gambling" element which cannot be ignored—the conscious acceptance of calculated and measured but nevertheless real risks, which involve an eventual recourse to last-minute improvisation—consider, for example, the way in which, in the weeks before the Congress of Berlin, he pondered and weighed up the possible attitude of France. These statesmanlike qualities inevitably have their counterpart; a complete cynicism in carrying out a policy which seems to be dictated by the national interest, but of which the author himself considers certain aspects scarcely honourable, and a certain contempt for human beings, such as appears in the treatment meted out to Wood, as much in 1878, when he was left in the most absolute ignorance, as in 1879 when he was shamefully "liquidated". But this policy, which only aimed at efficiency, compares favourably with Granville's policy which aimed at morality but was merely uncertain and groping, and finally accepted the fruits of "the immorality" of others. (This was seen, for example, in the decision to retain Cyprus taken at the beginning of Gladstone's Ministry.)

It is best to reserve judgement concerning the results of Salisbury's policy. Undoubtedly, experience has shown that the acquisition of Cyprus did not have the importance attributed to it by British statesmen in 1878; it neither gave a firm basis to British policy in the

Eastern Mediterranean, nor blocked the Russian advance in the Balkans and Anatolia (a preoccupation which was to lose its significance when Great Britain, at the beginning of the twentieth century, thought of a rapprochement with Russia). The haggling over Cyprus was the apex of a very complex diplomatic structure; it does not seem as if the facts justified the enterprise, and in particular that Cyprus had the strategic value assigned to her. It was doubtless difficult to foresee this in 1878, but what is definite is, that for a gain which in the event was illusory, Tunisian independence was sacrificed. In consenting to this, Salisbury broke sharply with the Tunisian policy which Palmerston had defined between 1835 and 1841 in his effort to avoid French expansion and to maintain the Mediterranean balance. The internationalization of the Turkish question (after 1856) and the agreement of the Powers for a controlled and limited partition of the Ottoman Empire gradually diminished the dangers which a French annexation of Tunisia could create for British interests in the Mediterranean. Salisbury's decision in 1878 was the result of an understanding of this new situation in the Mediterranean. At the moment when the Great Powers were embarking on world conquest, Palmerston's conception of Mediterranean balance was evidently obsolete. Seen from this angle, the occupation of Tunisia by France was merely the first episode of the great division of Africa among the Empires, which was to continue for forty years right up to the Treaty of Versailles, and in which Salisbury himself was to play a decisive role.

© ANDRÉ RAYMOND 1961

SA'AD ZAGHLUL AND THE BRITISH

By Elie Kedourie

WHEN SA'AD ZAGHLUL went to see Sir Reginald Wingate, the High
Commissioner in Egypt, on November 13, 1918, to ask for the complete independence of Egypt, he was already an old man with a
crowded political past behind him. He had been born, probably in
1857, in Ibiana, the son of a local well-to-do family with some official
connexions in the province; he had been sent to Cairo to study at
al-Azhar, and there became a disciple of Muhammad Abduh who made
him literary editor of the *Egyptian Gazette*, of which he remained the
editor for a few years, between the accession of Tawfiq Pasha to the
Khediviate and the fiasco of the 'Urabi rebellion. While he was literary
editor, Zaghlul contributed an article to the *Gazette* on constitutional
government, which provides a remarkable indication of the views he
then held, and with which both Egyptians and British continued to
associate him for many years later.

"The tyrant," wrote Zaghlul, "is usually defined as he who does what
he pleases irresponsibly, who rules as his passions incline him,
whether this agrees with the *Shar'*, or is contrary to it, whether it
conforms to the *Sunna* or differs from it. Because of this you see
that when people hear this vocable or something similar to it, they
attribute to it this meaning and are seized with displeasure at its
mention, owing to the great misfortunes they have derived from it,
and to the great damage it has done to peoples and nations. They
are justified in their displeasure and disgust because they have derived
from it nothing but misfortune and from its rule nothing but mis-
haps. They have indeed seen that tyranny makes souls perish unjustly, that it eats the possessions of men greedily, sheds blood without due cause, and brings utter destruction on the country. Therefore
men are not to be blamed if they are disinclined to praise it, even
though some might understand by it something which is not its
usual meaning.

"It is clear from what we have said above that the Divine Law does

139

not allow it, and that it makes mandatory the limitation of rule by tradition and law. But it is clear and obvious that the rules of the Divine Law by themselves cannot limit rule, because they are but concepts present in the mind of doctors and learned men, or else are indicated by means of symbols set down in books. They are not sufficient to control the ruler if he only has knowledge of them. For limitation of rule to be efficient, there must be men who actually conduct themselves according to its tenets, and who behave as these rules require, men who are ready to set right the ruler, should he deviate from the true path, to exhort him to keep to it and walk in its ways. It is for this reason that our Lord 'Umar, may God be pleased with him, asked the people, in his well-known address, to set him right whenever he erred in applying the rules of the noble *Shar'*, and for this reason God, the most high, said: 'Let there be formed among you a group who call for good deeds, who prescribe that which is customary to consider good, and who prohibit evil, and these shall prosper.' It cannot be denied that this noble verse calls generally on kings and others to do good, it orders them to follow what it is customary to consider good, and it forbids them the doing of evil, so that religion may be firmly based, and nobody trespass his prescribed bounds whether he rules or is ruled. This duty cannot be delegated, but is obligatory and incumbent on all, as the doctors have stated—it was made obligatory on the Muslim community that an *umma*—meaning a *ta'ifa* [group]—drawn from it should arise, whose duty would be to call for good actions, to prescribe that which it is customary to consider good, and to prohibit evil, in order that the Divine Law may be safeguarded, and in order that those who are tempted to transgress should not trespass its limits, and those with wayward passions should not haughtily disregard it."[1]

The article, with all its limitations of style and argument, is, for its time and place, a remarkable attempt to deduce the necessity of constitutional government from the prescriptions of Islam. Whether the attempt is convincing or not, the fact remains that Zaghlul continued to be associated with such views after the 'Urabi rebellion, when he became a lawyer with a private practice, and subsequently a judge in the Civil Courts. It was on the strength of these views, of his association with the disciples of Muhammad Abduh, and of his reputation

[1] The article is reproduced in Abbas Mahmud al-'Aqqad, *Sa'ad Zaghlul* (Cairo, 1936), pp. 65–6.

for uprightness and honesty, that Cromer chose him in 1906 to become Minister of Education. Cromer had a high regard for Muhammad Abduh, and considered that his disciples, whom he called "the Girondists of the Egyptian national movement",[2] were the only group with whom lay any hope of constitutional advance in Egypt. Zaghlul's advancement was thus a deliberate move to encourage this tendency in Egyptian politics, a move also to checkmate the Khedive Abbas Hilmi and circumscribe his authority over the Egyptian ministers. It was well-known at the time that the Khedive hated Muhammad Abduh, who had died in 1905, and it is reported that when he heard that some of his Court officials had attended Muhammad Abduh's funeral, he became very angry and said: "He is, as you know, the enemy of God, the enemy of the Prophet, the enemy of religion, the enemy of the Prince, the enemy of the *ulama*, the enemy of the Muslims, the enemy of his people, the enemy even of himself, why then show him such regard?"[3] The Khedive did not like Zaghlul's appointment, and subsequently came into conflict with him over the separate institution of a School of Religious Law, which would not be under the control of al-Azhar, a project which Zaghlul advocated and the Khedive opposed. He liked him even less when he suspected that Zaghlul, together with his brother Fathi, was instrumental in organizing *Hizb al-Umma*, the People's Party, a party which stood for constitutionalism and opposed the Khedive's autocratic leanings.[4] Zaghlul continued a minister for a number of years, and went out of office in 1912. While in office, and also out of it, he showed in public the same moderation which for Cromer was the hallmark of Muhammad Abduh's followers. Thus, in 1909, he was one of those who defended, against nationalist clamour, the extension of the Suez Canal Concession;[5] and when he stood for membership of the Legislative Assembly in 1913 his address to the electors of the Cairo constituency where he was a candidate confined itself to four points: he promised that, if elected, he would press for judicial reform, for educational reform, for municipal reform in Cairo, and that he would try to see that more attention was given to the needs of agriculture.[6]

[2] In his report on Egypt for 1905, Egypt No. 1 (1906), Cmd. 2817, *British Parliamentary Papers*, Vol. CXXXVII, 1906, pp. 15–16.

[3] Ahmad Shafiq Pasha, *Mudhakkirati fi nisf qarn* (*My memoirs of half a century*), (Cairo, 1936), Vol. II, Part 2, p. 72.

[4] Ahmad Shafiq, *op. cit.*, pp. 102, 112 and 129.

[5] C. C. Adams, *Islam and Modernism in Egypt* (London, 1933), p. 229.

[6] The address is printed in al-'Aqqad, pp. 154–5.

This was the reputation of the man who in November 1918 went with Abd al-'Aziz Fahmi and 'Ali Sha'rawi, both connected with the People's Party of pre-war days, to see Sir Reginald Wingate to demand Egyptian independence. It is true that, by then, he was definitely identified as a leader of the Opposition. In the Legislative Assembly, to which he had been elected in 1913, he had been made by his fellow-members elected Vice-President of the Assembly. In the short period before the Assembly was adjourned because of the outbreak of war, he had created a reputation for himself as a people's tribune and a stern critic of the Anglo-Egyptian administration, but always within moderate and reasonable bounds. His attitude seems to have reconciled the Khedive to him, and they became friendly; on the death of his father-in-law Mustafa Fahmi Pasha, the Khedive, who was in Constantinople, sent him a telegram of condolences which seems to have displeased the Residency; Husain Rushdi Pasha, the head of the Council of Ministers, reported to the Khedive that Mr Milne Cheetham had told him that the telegram created a bad impression because not only was it an encouragement to oppose the Administration, but could actually be considered as inciting to opposition.[7] During the war, Zaghlul made no public move, but in 1917, Sultan Fuad, who had just come to the throne, asked that he and Abd al-'Aziz Fahmi should be made ministers. The British Government refused, and thereafter Zaghlul and Abd al-'Aziz Fahmi constituted with a few others what has been called the King's *officine nocturne*.[8] These facts were, of course, not publicly known, and Zaghlul's reputation remained as that of an independent opposition-minded politician.

Zaghlul's visit to him, as Wingate well knew, could not but have been concerted with the Sultan and his ministers. Fuad's accession to the Sultanate had been unexpected. But for the deposition of Abbas Hilmi, the early death of his successor Husain Kamil, and the unacceptability of Husain Kamil's son to the British Government, Fuad would not have become Sultan. He therefore had a position to make secure and consolidate, an authority to sustain and increase, and this in the face of Abbas Hilmi's still unextinguished claim to the throne, his ministers' greater experience of affairs, and of a British control which, since the outbreak of war, had become ever more burdensome and meticulous. When they chose him to become Sultan, the authorities

[7] Ahmad Shafiq, *op. cit.*, pp. 272 and 350. In a note written in April 1919 (*Wingate Papers*), Sir Ronald Graham alleged that in 1914 Zaghlul was acting as the Khedive's agent in the Legislative Assembly.

[8] Sir Ronald Wingate, *Wingate of the Sudan* (London, 1955), pp. 225–6.

had considered him to be "at any rate not Anglophobe in his sympathies",[9] but even the most Anglophil Sultan, placed in Fuad's position, would have been bound, sooner or later, in attempting to consolidate his position, to create difficulties for the Occupying Power. His demand that Zaghlul and Abd al-'Aziz Fahmi should replace two ministers with whom he professed dissatisfaction, his creation of a circle of counsellors, deliberating behind the backs of his ministers,[10] his professed dissatisfaction with his Chief Minister, Husain Rushdi Pasha,[11] were all straws in the wind. As peace approached, barely a month before Zaghlul's fateful interview, Fuad again reiterated to Wingate his dissatisfaction with his ministers, and gave expression to his desire for Home Rule for Egypt on the lines of President Wilson's Fourteen Points. In reporting this interview to London, Wingate expressed the opinion that the motive of Fuad's behaviour was fear of the ex-Khedive and his family.[12] Again, exactly a week before Zaghlul's interview, Fuad spoke to Wingate of his desire for a purely Egyptian ministry, for a national assembly, and for a constitutional monarchy.[13] It is most unlikely that Fuad, in holding this language to Wingate, was moved by a sincere desire to diminish the legally unlimited prerogatives of the Sultanate. What is more likely is that he saw in Zaghlul's move, which he no doubt hoped to control and use for his own ends, a means of increasing his stature in the eyes of the Egyptians, and his power in those of the English, just as Abbas Hilmi had done in the case of Mustafa Kamil and his nationalist party, before he broke with them in 1904. This is all the more likely in that Fuad was, as Austen Chamberlain later described him, and as his career showed him to be, "sly, scheming, corrupt and autocratic".[14] Wingate himself, reporting at the end of 1917 some highly uncomplimentary remarks which Isma'il Sirri Pasha had made concerning Fuad, gave it as his opinion that Fuad was an autocrat.[15] In this autocrat invoking the Fourteen Points, then, we see the first partner in the prolonged game of chess which lasted from

[9] Lord Lloyd, *Egypt since Cromer* (London, 1933), Vol. I, p. 259.

[10] Wingate reported that the ministers did not like these proceedings: *Wingate Papers*, Wingate to Sir Ronald Graham, June 9, 1918. I am grateful to Mr. R. L. Hill and to the School of Oriental Studies, Durham University, for allowing me to consult the Wingate Papers.

[11] *Ibid.*, Wingate to Graham, March 24, 1918.

[12] *Ibid.*, Wingate to Hardinge, October 19, 1918.

[13] *Ibid.*, Wingate to Hardinge, November 6, 1918.

[14] Sir Charles Petrie, *Life and Letters of Sir Austen Chamberlain* (London, 1940), Vol. II, p. 341.

[15] *Wingate Papers*, Wingate to Graham, September 12, 1917.

1919 to 1922, when Allenby, extorting his famous Declaration from a reluctant Government in London, began the long, painful, humiliating liquidation of the British position in Egypt, which ended at last in the unlikely events of November 1956.

Zaghlul was acting in concert not only with Fuad, but with his ministers as well. These ministers, the principal of whom were Husain Rushdi and 'Adli Yeghen, had been in office since the outbreak of war. They had shown loyalty to the Occupying Power, had acquiesced in the deposition of Abbas and the declaration of the Protectorate, and had done their best to comply with the needs of the military. Now that Fuad was on the throne, that peace was about to return, they found their situation extremely weakened. They could be attacked for subservience to the British, for disloyalty to the Ottoman suzerain of Egypt and to the ex-Khedive, and they had to take action to protect themselves and to parry the attacks that were bound to come. So that, even if they had had no desire to claim independence, once they found Zaghlul and Fuad engaging on such a tactic, willy-nilly they had to follow suit and associate themselves with their demands. But, in any case, they themselves had cause for complaint and a desire to change the modalities of the Protectorate as these had developed in the years from 1914 to 1918.

In 1914 Kitchener was Consul-General. When war broke out he was on leave in London, and was persuaded to remain there and become Secretary of State for War during the hostilities. But the war was not thought likely to last very long, and Kitchener did not want to abandon his Egyptian post. This was why Sir Henry MacMahon, an Indian civilian, who had just retired from the position of Political Secretary to the Government of India, was appointed High Commissioner—as the British representative came to be known after the declaration of the Protectorate—as a stop-gap measure, and to keep the post open for Kitchener. MacMahon had spent all his official life in British India and had no intimate knowledge of Egypt. Now Egypt was not India. India was ruled by a tightly-knit, compact civil service, in which there was an unbroken chain of command from the District Officer in his remote province, to the central seat of authority in Delhi; Egypt under British Occupation, on the other hand, was a much more complicated and delicate mechanism to operate. While there could, of course, be no question that the last word lay with the British representative, yet his authority was not and could not be exercised directly. There was the Khedive, who was the legal ruler of the country, there were his ministers who were supposed to control and direct the native officials; these

ministers were flanked by British Advisers at the centre, and their sub-
ordinates by British Inspectors in the provinces: it was by means of this
peculiar dyarchy that the views and desires of the Occupying Power
were supposed to be transmitted and enforced. This meant that the
British representative had to manage and humour Khedive, ministers
and other official persons, and that his position precluded him from that
direct exercise of authority which, in a hierarchical civil service such
as that of British India, was customary as between superior and subordinate. The declaration of the Protectorate, the coming of MacMahon,
the concentration of large bodies of British and Allied troops in Egypt
—events all of them precipitated by the outbreak of war—could not
but exercise the greatest influence on the modes of British control of
Egypt; and this, in turn, could not but greatly disturb the Egyptian
ministers and official classes, accustomed as they had been to the
political and administrative traditions which had grown up from 1882
to 1914. In a private note written in October 1919, Sir Reginald
Wingate recorded an interview he had with Sultan Husain Kamil,
while MacMahon was still High Commissioner, in which the Sultan
bitterly complained of the increased powers of the British officials, and
stated that Egypt was then being ruled by a *camorra*,[16] of which they
were the head. From the same note it appears that the Sultan complained to Lord Hardinge, who was passing through Egypt, and that
his complaint, coinciding with Kitchener's death, resulted in Sir
Reginald Wingate, then Governor-General of the Sudan, being appointed to replace MacMahon.[17] Writing to Hardinge shortly after
assuming his new office, Wingate described how Lord Edward Cecil,
the Financial Adviser, had been given great authority by MacMahon,
and how everybody, British and Egyptian, was looking up to him for
advancement and promotion.[18] MacMahon, it would seem, used
Cecil as a kind of prime minister.

Such, then, were the factors influencing the ministers' behaviour
when they supported Zaghlul's request that an Egyptian delegation
proceed to London to discuss the grant of Egyptian independence. In
this matter it would seem that Zaghlul, free of official responsibilities,
was able to set the pace, and that the ministers, whether they liked it or
not, had to endorse his demands. As for themselves, it is doubtful
whether they really wanted full independence, or whether—which is

[16] *Camorra:* Secret society in Naples (Oxford Concise Dictionary).
[17] *Wingate Papers: Note on the Main Points which have given rise to the Present
Situation in Egypt,* October 1919.
[18] *Ibid.,* Wingate to Hardinge, January 31, 1917.

the likelier case—they would have been content with a definition of the Protectorate which would circumscribe the authority of the British officials, and allow the Egyptian ministers more elbow-room. In a moving and eloquent Note which he wrote for Wingate in December 1918, Husain Rushdi declared that the Protectorate was a label which could be used to designate either outright annexation, or a reconciliation of British and Egyptian interests. He wanted to know which it was to be; this was the purpose of the talks which they wanted to hold with the British Government in London, and he disclaimed any desire to make the Egyptian question international, or to seek to present it before the Peace Conference.[19] If this was Husain Rushdi's view, the views of the other Egyptians concerned in Zaghlul's move of November were, at the outset, hardly more clear-cut. Fuad, it is safe to say, had started something, and was waiting to see how the cat would jump; he had been careful not to commit himself publicly in any way, and at the worst, had only to disclaim responsibility, and to say that it was the fault of his ministers, of Zaghlul, of public opinion . . .; if, however, the British were ready to parley, he would put himself at the head of the movement, and so manœuvre as to obtain the greatest benefits for himself and his house. If such was the calculation, he was to be sorely disappointed, to find that in Zaghlul he had an old, wily partner, and that the forces he helped to unleash were no longer under his control. As for Zaghlul and his unofficial associates, they also seem to have ventured hopefully, without really knowing the true extent of their demands, or what they would consider a satisfactory outcome. This was the attitude of Ahmad Lutfi al-Sayyid who was a member of Zaghlul's group, which soon came to be known as the *Wafd*. He told Muhammad Husain Haikal at the time that the plan, as he saw it, was for Zaghlul's *Wafd* to proceed to Paris and lay the Egyptian demands before the Peace Conference; if they succeeded in this, well and good; if not, then Husain Rushdi and 'Adli Yeghen would go to London on their own and endeavour to make precise the conditions of the protectorate, and to set up a true constitutional government for the country.[20] Whether these were the precise views of Zaghlul himself, we do not know, but his subsequent behaviour would indicate that he was a man ready to extract the maximum benefit from any favourable opportunity.

The counter-move by the British Government to Zaghlul's move

[19] *Wingate Papers:* Note by Husain Rushdi Pasha, December 13, 1918.
[20] Muhammad Husain Haikal, *Mudhakkirat* . . . (*Memoirs* . . .) (Cairo, 1951), Vol. I, p. 82.

came quickly. It was a categorical refusal. No Egyptian leader, official or unofficial, was to move out of Egypt, to go either to Paris or London; further, Wingate was rebuked for allowing himself to be trapped into receiving Zaghlul's delegation and allowing them to make these demands.[21] The rebuke was less than just, for Wingate had given plenty of warning of the true situation in Egypt, and he could hardly have refused, unless he were to behave like an oriental despot, to receive three men as prominent in Egyptian society as Zaghlul and his two friends; it was, further, Cromer's policy, and a tradition which he bequeathed to his successors of whom Wingate was one of the worthiest, that the British representative in Egypt was accessible to all classes of men, and ready to look into and redress the grievances of the most insignificant of Egyptians. It would also seem that the refusal of Zaghlul's request was misconceived. If Zaghlul, the ministers and the Sultan were acting in concert, and if they maintained a united front, what then would the British Government do? For, then, it would come to a trial of strength; were they prepared for it? There is no indication that the consequences of refusal were seriously considered. For not only was Zaghlul himself refused permission to go to Europe, the ministers themselves were forbidden to do so. It might be that, had they been allowed to go to London, as Wingate himself urged that they should, they would have been adroit enough to take the initiative away from Zaghlul, and thus enable the British Government to break the united front which Zaghlul, the ministers and the Sultan maintained, each for his own particular ends. But it is doubtful whether they would have been adroit enough, or daring enough, to proceed on their own, while knowing that the Sultan would be obscurely manœuvring behind their backs, and Zaghlul ready to denounce any settlement in which he did not have a part. In the event, faced with the British refusal, they resigned, and were soon declaring that they would not go to London without Zaghlul, obviously fearing that if they left him in Egypt, he would be in a strong position to outbid them.[22]

The ministers were prevailed upon to hold back their resignation for the time being, but Wingate found himself in a difficult position, between an equivocating Sultan alternately saying that Zaghlul and his friends were justified in their demands, and his ministers right to resign, and then again saying that the ministers were indispensable and should be prevailed upon to stay in office, and that he himself had no sympathy

[21] Ronald Wingate, *op. cit.*, p. 234.
[22] *Wingate Papers:* Residency, Cairo, to Foreign Office, telegram January 11, 1919.

with Zaghlul but dare not disown him, and ministers, in part gen-
uinely offended by London's behaviour, and again in part fearful of
seeming less extreme than Zaghlul.[23] All the while, Zaghlul, now in
the limelight, together with his committee, was organizing opposition
to the Occupying Power. The text of a petition asking that Zaghlul and
his delegation be allowed to travel to Europe to present the Egyptian
case was spread throughout the land and signatures collected for it. The
provincial authorities, acting on the instructions of the Ministry of the
Interior, attempted to confiscate these petitions. Zaghlul, in what may
have been a concerted move,[24] protested to Husain Rushdi against the
confiscations. What followed throws light not only on the course of
the so-called Egyptian Revolution of 1919, but on the quality of the
British administration of Egypt in those years. Husain Rushdi went
with the protest to the Adviser of the Ministry of the Interior and asked
him what reply should be made. The Adviser was then Mr Haines,
who had been an Inspector and then a Chief Collector of Taxes; he
had been made Adviser to the Interior by MacMahon on Lord Edward
Cecil's advice. "In this post," writes Lord Lloyd, "he displayed little
of his former zeal or competence, and refused to listen to any sort of
criticism or advice, thus cutting off the High Commissioner from his
chief source of information."[25] Mr Haines, as he explained to Wingate,
now told Husain Rushdi to answer Zaghlul by saying that the petitions
were being confiscated by the order of the Adviser of the Ministry of
the Interior.[26] Husain Rushdi replied in this sense; the letter was made
public, and it was plain for all to see that the Sultan's ministers had no
part or lot in putting down Zaghlul's movement. But this dissociation
of the Egyptian ministers from their British advisers, facilitated by
Haines's extraordinary move, was not the only sign by which the
ministers conveyed their approval of Zaghlul's movement. There is
evidence to show that they took positive steps to facilitate his work.
The petition had been sent, writes Muhammad Husain Haikal, to
lawyers, doctors, engineers and other professional people: "for these,
it was not difficult to sign the petitions, since their culture and their
appreciation of the meaning of independence were enough to make
them eager to sign. But copies of the petition had also been sent to
local elected bodies, such as provincial councils, and to 'umdahs and
notables, and lo and behold, thousands and hundreds of thousands of

[23] *Wingate Papers*: Wingate to Balfour, December 5, 1918; Wingate to
Graham, December 22; note of meeting with Sultan, January 1, 1919.
[24] This is what al-'Aqqad states, *op. cit.*, p. 205.   [25] *Op. cit.*, Vol. I, p. 281.
[26] *Wingate Papers*: Haines to Wingate, November 25, 1918.

these signatures began to come in from every side; this is because
Rushdi Pasha's ministry enouraged the *mudirs* and the *ma'murs*, and
made them encourage people who were afraid of the power of Government, to sign the petitions."[27] Ahmad Shafiq Pasha, in his *Survey of
Egyptian Politics*, also mentions that the government exerted its influence on behalf of Zaghlul's movement and confirms his argument by a
speech which Husain Rushdi made a few years after these events re-
counting the help which he gave to the *Wafd* while in office.[28] It was
not only the ministers, but the Palace as well which exerted its influence in the same direction; so Abd al-Khaliq Tharwat—one of Husain
Rushdi's fellow-ministers who, it seems, had not been consulted about
the resignation[29]—told Sir Walter Brunyate, the Judicial Adviser,
adding that false rumours were being spread by the Palace Staff.[30] A
curious effect of these tactics emerges from the story told in a note
by Sir Ronald Graham on *Unrest in Egypt* to the effect that an influential provincial notable loyal to the British connexion told a British
Inspector that he had subscribed £10,000 to Zaghlul's movement because he understood it had the support of the British, and that he gladly
cancelled his subscription when he learnt to the contrary.[31] Later, in
the disturbances which followed the banishment of Zaghlul and his
friends, some provincial officials took the part of the rioters, others
remained passive, the police in some places showed indiscipline, and
in at least one recorded instance Egyptian troops incited the mob to
destruction.[32] It would seem, then, that the Egyptian Revolution of
1919 was, at least in instigation, and at the beginning, a revolution
directed from above.

While effervescence was mounting in the country, Wingate was

[27] *Op. cit.*, Vol. I, p. 86.

[28] Ahmad Shafiq, *Hauliyyat Misr al-Siyasiyya, Tamhid (Annual Survey of
Egyptian Politics, Introduction)*, (Cairo, 1926), Vol. I, p. 177.

[29] *Wingate Papers*: Residency, Cairo, to Foreign Office, telegram December 5,
1918.

[30] *Ibid.*, Brunyate to Wingate, December 15, 1918.

[31] *Ibid.*, Note on *Unrest in Egypt* by Sir Ronald Graham, April 9, 1919.

[32] The instances are found in Tawwaf, pseud., *Egypt, 1919* (Alexandria, 1925),
who records incidents in Bani Suef and Aswan; in Ahmad Shafiq, *Hauliyyat,
Tamhid*, Vol. I, p. 508, who records the arrest of the vice-governor of Minia
Province, its director of the Parquet and judge, who were accused of rebellion
against the government; and in a note sent by a notable of Bani Mazar to Milner
while he was in Egypt with his Mission, which records with circumstantial detail
the incitement of a government official, who encouraged the people to attack
British troops. Cf. *Milner Papers*: I am grateful to the Librarian of New College,
Oxford, for allowing me to consult these Papers.

endeavouring to make the British Government change its policy, and make some less categorically negative reply to the Egyptian ministers. The Government went so far as to say that they would, some time, discuss the issue with Husain Rushdi and his colleagues, but that Zaghlul was, on no account, to move out of Egypt. But early in the crisis Husain Rushdi and 'Adli had declared that they would not go without Zaghlul, so when the final reply of the British Government was given to them, they made their resignation public, on March 1, 1919. Wingate was then in London, having gone there to convince Curzon of his views, and Sir Milne Cheetham was in charge at the Residency. He sent reports which represented Zaghlul and his ministerial sympathizers as having lost popularity, and the country as quiet and peaceful.[33] When the ministers' resignation was made known, Zaghlul acted at once. He visited the Palace and left a minatory letter for the Sultan. "We know," the letter said, "that Your Highness may have been compelled by family reasons to accept the throne, but the nation, on the other hand, believes that Your acceptance of the throne during the temporary and illegal Protectorate—out of regard for those family circumstances—should not turn Your Highness away from working for the independence of Your country. People, therefore, have wondered how Your Highness's counsellors did not pay regard to the nation in this difficult period. The nation asks that Your Highness be the first one to come to its help in attaining independence, however much this might cost Your Highness. How can it have escaped Your Highness's counsellors that the terms of Rushdi Pasha's resignation do not allow any honourable and patriotic Egyptian to take his place? How can it have escaped them that a ministry formed on a programme contrary to the will of the people is doomed to failure? We do not advise our Lord falsely when we beg Him to acquaint Himself with the opinion of His nation before taking a final decision concerning the present ministry. To stand between the nation and its demands is a responsibility which the counsellors of our Lord have not scrutinized with the requisite precision."[34] The erstwhile member of the *officine nocturne* was giving notice to his coadjutor that he could not so easily wriggle out of his schemes, that even if he were tempted to give in to the obstinacy of the British, Zaghlul would not allow it. Cromer's girondist was turning jacobin.

[33] His despatch of February 24, 1919, is quoted in Lloyd, *op. cit.*, Vol. I, pp. 290-1.

[34] Quoted in Ahmad Baha' al-Din, *Ayam laha tarikh* (*Historic Days*), (Cairo, [1954], 1959 ed.), p. 113.

Faced with these threats which might prevent the formation of a government, Cheetham deported Zaghlul and his principal lieutenants to Malta. Revolution thereupon broke out in Egypt: mobs in Cairo, Alexandria and the principal provincial cities, telegraph wires cut, rail-tracks destroyed, Englishmen killed. Wingate was in London with Curzon, while Lloyd George and Balfour were in Paris. They decided to take some kind of drastic action. Allenby was in Paris; there and then they appointed him Special High Commissioner and charged him with restoring order in Egypt; Wingate they left high and dry in London. Allenby was appointed on March 20 and he reached Egypt on March 25. But two days before his appointment, on March 18, Balfour in Paris sent some instructions concerning Egypt which, taken together with the way in which Allenby chose to apply them, were to have a fateful influence on subsequent events. On that day Balfour conceded Husain Rushdi's demands that in any negotiations with the British Government, Zaghlul should accompany the ministers. To this demand, so long resisted by the British Government, Balfour now declared that he had no objection.[35] What reasonable negotiation had failed to achieve, violence now seemed forcefully to obtain. Here is yet another instance of the ruinous consequences which the war and the peace negotiations had on the machinery of British government in those crucial years; for it is hardly to be credited that such a proceeding would have been possible, had the British ministers and their advisers not been scattered between London and Paris, rushed, harried and intolerably overworked.

Fortified by such instructions and thinking to pacify Egypt, Allenby now released Zaghlul whom he regarded, as he informed the Foreign Office, as representing the opinion of the majority of Egyptian intel-lectuals,[36] and allowed him to go to Paris where he spent his time writing ineffective memoranda to the Powers and bickering with his friends. Egypt, which Allenby had hoped to tranquillize, remained effervescent, for the remedy was, of course, worse than the disease. Now that the British had given way to violence, violence must con-tinue. Hence, civil service strikes, riots, demonstrations, shootings, and that general unsettlement which pervades an oriental country when it knows its master to be weak and hesitant. To make matters worse, the British Government in London appointed a Mission of Enquiry under Lord Milner which, instead of going immediately to Egypt, waited until December before doing so. By that time, the agitation had

[35] *Wingate Papers:* Balfour, Paris, to Foreign Office, London, telegram March 18, 1919.   [36] *Wingate Papers:* Allenby to Foreign Office, April 20, 1919.

increased enormously and a campaign, which proved successful, was
started, the purpose of which was to convince and intimidate Egyptians into boycotting the Mission. The Mission came, looked, listened
and held talks in private, while the appearance, or the suspected appearance, of any of its members in public led to demonstrations, riots and
murderous attacks on Egyptians suspected of a desire for compromise.[37] It left after three months. It found that the deadlock could not
be broken, and conciliatory statements only made it more intractable
than ever. The reason was quite simple: Zaghlul had triumphed over
the British Government in March 1919, and however futile was his
present stay in Paris, no politician found the courage to conclude an
agreement to which he was not a party, and would therefore feel at
liberty to denounce. For Zaghlul had by now been invested with a
martyr's aura, he was the leader and the father of his people, and however much they disliked him, his rivals did not find it in them to stand
up and denounce him. In this, of course, Zaghlul had the advantage
over them, for his ambition gave him a force of spirit, a frenzy which
cowed and intimidated better, more honest, but less forceful men. The
blunders of his Egyptian rivals, as of the British Government, of course
gave him many opportunities, but it was his character which enabled
him to seize these opportunities and shape them to his own ends.

The straits to which the British Government were now reduced may
be summed up in this, that they now had to treat on equal terms with
men whom, before 1914, they were accustomed to manage, with men,
moreover, who, unused to the rough and tumble of real politics, were
bound, in any negotiation, to prove broken reeds. They had to treat
with courtiers, with obedient bureaucrats, with tame and sage adminis-
trators who, at the slightest squall, were likely to scurry for safety. All,
that is, except Zaghlul. So in the end, the Milner Mission were confronted by the inescapable conclusion that if Muhammad would not
go to the mountain, the mountain had to come to Muhammad. To
Zaghlul they must go, and to Zaghlul they went. The suggestion
apparently came from Husain Rushdi, who told the Mission that the
only people qualified to speak on behalf of Egypt were Zaghlul and
his *Wafd* in Paris.[38] It was arranged for Zaghlul and his friends to visit
London and talk with the Milner Mission in the summer of 1920. The
talks were private, and were in no way to implicate the British Government. In particular, any proposal that Milner would make, would be

[37] See J. A. Spender, *Life, Journalism and Politics* (London, 1927), Vol. II, pp.
93–5, for his experiences in Egypt as a member of the Mission.
[38] Muhammad Husain Haikal, *op. cit.*, Vol. I, p. 100.

on his own responsibility; as Lord Curzon later said: ". . . it was made perfectly clear at the time . . . that these were the views of Lord Milner and his colleagues. It was stated that the Government had not considered them."[39] The negotiations, in which Zaghlul showed himself resourceful and obstinate, issued in a document. "This document, which presently came to be known as the Milner-Zaghlul Agreement, but which," the Milner Report notes with a fine discrimination, "on the face of it, was not an agreement, but merely an outline of the bases on which an agreement might subsequently be framed,"[40] abandoned all the British positions which had been erected in defence of the Protectorate. It conceded that a treaty should be concluded between Great Britain and Egypt, "under which Great Britain will recognize the independence of Egypt as a constitutional monarchy with representative institutions".[41] It is a strange spectacle, that of Lord Milner in his old age, slowly coming to adore that which, in his South African days, he was intent, with such stoic resolution, on burning. The analysis of the Egyptian situation which his report presented has been subjected, by Lord Lloyd, to severe but just criticism.[42] Here, it remains to add that Lord Milner's vision of future Anglo-Egyptian relations was, for so experienced a statesman, fanciful and sentimental. He believed that the agreement which was not an agreement, which he had negotiated with Zaghlul, would ensure lasting peace and amity with Egypt. "My belief," he said in the House of Lords, "is that a course of action is possible which will enable us to ensure all that we need in Egypt, including the maintenance of order and progress of which we ourselves are the authors, without involving ourselves in permanent hostility with the Egyptian nation. My intimate conviction is that, while there is undoubtedly an element of Egyptian nationalism which is anti-British, the better and stronger elements of it are not anti-British but simply pro-Egyptian. . . ."[43] If only these "better and stronger" elements were encouraged and appeased, so he believed, the whole problem would be solved. So he declared in a letter of September 16, 1920, in reply to Churchill's criticism of his proposals to Zaghlul, which had by then become public.[44] The "blessed" word, independence, he said, would get the British Government round its difficulty, just as the "unfortunate" word, Protectorate, was now the

[39] H.L. Debs., 5th series, November 4, 1920, col. 196.

[40] Egypt No. 1 (1921), Cmd. 1131, British Parliamentary Papers, Vol. XLII, 1921, p. 23.

[41] Cmd. 1131 (1921), p. 24.   [42] Lloyd, op. cit., Vol. II, pp. 17–22.

[43] H.L. Debs., November 4, 1920, col. 213.   [44] Milner Papers.

source of all the troubles. Belief in the magic power of words comes strangely from this old proconsul. Another facet of his attitude shows with startling clarity that failure of nerve, that weakening of the will to rule, which began to afflict the British ruling classes in the aftermath of the first World War, and which was to make the dissolution of the British Empire so ugly and ruinous, to subjects and rulers alike. J. A. Spender, his colleague on the Mission, has recorded that Milner's view, then, "was that if the Egyptians did not want us to govern them and could keep order and maintain solvency without us, we were under no obligation to undertake the invidious, difficult and very expensive task of governing them against their will".[45] That such was his view is confirmed by a conversation he had with a European business man in Egypt in January 1920. Since Great Britain's interests in Egypt were few, what sense was there with continuing the attempt to govern Egypt at great cost in men and money? He admitted that British government was in the interests of the Egyptian masses, that they probably wished it to continue, but they were mute, and the only clamour to be heard was that of the politicians abusing and reviling the British. In these conditions, he confessed, Great Britain would have neither the power nor the will to go on ruling.[46]

Holding such views, it is logical that Milner should have made the kind of agreement he did with Zaghlul. But the agreement was yet not an agreement. Zaghlul argued that since it did not fulfil all the demands that he had been mandated to pursue, it was necessary for him, before finally committing himself, to go back to his principals, the Egyptian people, and seek their approval. He was allowed to get away with this monstrous argument, and he retired to take the waters in France, with Milner's concessions in his pocket, and himself uncommitted. But he felt he could do better; with a little management, he would probably be able to improve his terms, and to emerge as the one undisputed leader. He despatched his agents to "consult" the Egyptian people, and accompanied them with a secret letter to his supporters in Egypt, Hafiz 'Afifi, Wissa Wasif, and Mustafa al-Nahhas, explaining that whatever these agents might say in support of Milner's proposals, he himself was against them; he knew, he said, that his colleagues, in a compromising spirit which he fully understood, wished the agreement ratified, but he himself preferred to go on with the struggle rather than accept a diminished Egyptian sovereignty.[47]

[45] Spender, *op. cit.*, p. 91.   [46] *Milner Papers.*
[47] Text of Zaghlul's letter of August 22, 1920, in Ahmad Shafiq, *Hauliyyat, Tamhid*, Vol. I, pp. 746–7.

He went further. 'Adli Yeghen had acted, on Zaghlul's request, as intermediary in the talks between him and Milner. Zaghlul now said that but for 'Adli, he would have obtained much better terms. His follower, al-Nahhas, sent a telegram from France in November 1920 to Amin al-Rafi'i, the editor of the nationalist newspaper, *al-Akhbar*, which said that 'Adli had been a disaster for the Wafd.[48] It is therefore not surprising that the "consultation" came to nothing, and Milner was informed that he had to concede more. He gave up at that stage, and his Report, together with the details of his negotiations with Zaghlul, was published in the spring of 1921. Allenby reported at the time that the Egyptians were astounded at the extent of the British concessions, but he pointed out that the British Government was now committed to them.[49] This indeed was the case; no agreement had emerged from Milner's negotiations, and yet the British were committed to concessions which should have been the outcome of a hard-and-fast treaty. The vexing prospect was that negotiations would have to begin all over again, and other concessions probably made.

To get on with these negotiations, 'Adli formed a new ministry; but Zaghlul was now in Egypt and on the rampage. Though he was not in the Government, he claimed the right to head the Egyptian delegation which was starting out for London. Not unnaturally, 'Adli refused such a humiliating proposal, and Zaghlul started attacking him as a British agent and a traitor to his country. Riots and demonstrations again inflamed the country; one particularly bloody affray took place in Alexandria on May 20 and 21, in which foreigners were murdered and their houses looted. The events of this riot were minutely documented by a commission of enquiry, whose report is a classic of its kind.[50] From this report it is possible to form an accurate idea of the methods of Zaghlul's political organization. At the outset of the riots, the following circular was distributed among the populace:

"You have known who are the members of the official delegation. They are the lowest of God's creatures on God's earth. They are people who have neither conscience nor honour. They are people who sacrifice their honour for the sake of filling their bellies and for filling governmental positions. Where are your students? Where are your fellaheen? Where are your devotees? Where is he who offers

[48] Ahmad Shafiq, *op. cit.*, p. 850.
[49] *Wingate Papers*: Allenby to Foreign Office, April 16, 1921.
[50] Egypt No. 3 (1921), Cmd. 1527, *British Parliamentary Papers*, Vol. XLII, 1921.

himself to redeem his homeland and save his country from disaster?
Let you be rising. Rise, you heroes, and generously give what is
dear and cheap for the sake of your Fatherland, and for the consoli-
dation of the throne of the nation and its faithful agent Sa'ad Pasha
Zaghlul. Know ye that heavenly laws and worldly laws allow killing
and shedding of blood in this circumstance. Let the Prophet—may
Allah bless Him!—be the best example. He killed many in the way
of spreading the Mohammedan call and exterminating the influence
of *murtaddin* [backsliders], and the night resembles the preced-
ing night. We defend the dearest thing on earth; defend our life
or death; defend our children and grandchildren. Remember the
Prophet's word, 'The love of home is part of the faith'.
"What have you decided upon? History is on the alert.
"Long live Saad! No chief except Saad!
Down with the Government's Delegation!
Down with the dissentient members!"[51]

The follower of Muhammad Abduh then, the believer in constitutionalism and reform, found that he had, in pursuit of power, to resort
to religious fanaticism and to appeal to the savage instincts of the mob.
He does not seem to have flinched. Cromer foresaw it all when he said
in his Report for 1906 that whilst some enlightened Egyptians might
wish to divorce politics from religion, yet "[unless] they can convince
the Moslem masses of their militant Islamism, they will fail to arrest
their attention or attract their sympathy. Appeals," he went on, "either
overt or covert, to racial and religious passions are thus a necessity of their existence in order to insure the furtherance of their programme."[52] We may add that Zaghlul's organization not only appealed
to the passions of the mob, but found it useful to use terrorism and
political murder. The Report on Egypt for 1920 records the arrest,
trial, and death sentence, of Abd al-Rahman Fahmi, the secretary of
the Wafd, and of his accomplices, who were charged with and con-
victed of a conspiracy to assassinate ministers and overthrow the
government.[53] Again, in the wake of Sir Lee Stack's murder at the end
of 1924, the terrorist gang which executed him was discovered and
found to be led by a Wafdist deputy.

Disregarding Zaghlul's clamour, 'Adli went to negotiate. The talks

in London dragged on until the end of the year when 'Adli, feeling that
he could not go back with an agreement, unless he could offer something much better than what Zaghlul had already obtained, broke
them off, returned to Egypt and resigned. It was then that Allenby
decided to take matters in his own hands. He was impatient with the
Government in London, and surrounded by advisers, of whom Sir
Gilbert Clayton, the Acting Adviser to the Interior, Sir Sheldon Amos,
the Acting Judicial Adviser, and Patterson, the Acting Financial Adviser, were the most prominent, who advocated the same policy as
Milner's for the settlement of Anglo-Egyptian relations. As early as
April 1919, Clayton was writing to Sir Reginald Wingate that Egyptian national aspirations had to be satisfied.[54] On November 17, 1921,
the Residency in Cairo transmitted to London a memorandum
in which these three Advisers, joined by Dowson, the Educational
Adviser, declared that unless the principle of Egyptian independence
were conceded, serious revolution would break out in Egypt. The
Advisers were, of course, justified in saying that the Egyptians had
formed certain expectations on the basis of the apparent policy of the
British Government, but had they not exceeded their function in
giving the impression to various Ministers, as they say they undoubtedly did, that "a policy of liberal concessions would be adopted"?
They were now asking the British Government to make their words
come true, and they offered to ease the process for it by assuring it that
a liberal policy could be elaborated on the spot, "and a Ministry
formed to carry it out even if no Egyptian Minister is prepared today
to sign official convention containing that programme as full satisfaction of Egyptian claims"![55] The meaning of these dark hints was
made clear when Allenby proceeded in the following weeks to deport
Zaghlul to the Seychelles and to press on the British Government, with
all the vehemence at his command, a policy whereby Great Britain
would unilaterally concede Egyptian independence, only reserving to
itself four subjects relating to imperial communications, to the Sudan,
to foreign residents in Egypt, and to Egyptian defence. This scheme, it
appears, was put together with the Advisers, and with some Egyptian
politicians who were Zaghlul's rivals. Isma'il Sidqi Pasha has even
claimed that it was he who produced the first draft of the scheme.[56]

[54] *Wingate Papers:* Clayton to Wingate, April 21, 1919.
[55] Egypt No. 1 (1922), Cmd. 1592, *British Parliamentary Papers*, Vol. XXIII,
1922, pp. 5–6.
[56] Isma'il Sidqi Pasha, *Mudhakkirati (My Memoirs)*, (Cairo, 1950), pp. 25–6.
In his despatch of January 12, 1922, Allenby admitted that his scheme was

Can it be, as Lloyd suspected, that Allenby had engaged himself beyond recall to these Egyptians, and that this explains the minatory and urgent tone of his despatches to London? For the British Government did not at all like his proposals, and asked for Amos and Clayton to be sent to London to explain them. Allenby countered that this would be of no use, and insisted: "If, on the other hand, they were rejected, he held out a prospect of endless trouble."[57] To clinch the matter, he himself, in the end, went to London, and wrung approval from Lloyd George and Curzon. The spectacle is curious and alarming. "The Bull"—as he was known—a forceful soldier, knowing his own mind, indignant at the behaviour of dithering, equivocating "frocks", decides to force the issue. He descends on London, and to Curzon's polite enquiry after Lady Allenby, replies: "I have left her behind in Egypt, as I feared there might be trouble if I brought her away." The politicians go on talking, and he gets impatient: "Well," he says to Lloyd George, "it is no good disputing any longer. I have told you what I think is necessary. I have waited five weeks for a decision, and I can't wait any longer: I shall tell Lady Allenby to come home." He was, it seems, not mistaken in his view of the politicians: Lloyd George, hearing the ultimatum, rises and puts his hand on Allenby's arm. "You have waited five weeks, Lord Allenby," he says, "wait five more minutes."[58]

Allenby got his Declaration; the basis of a lasting settlement it was to be. Tharwat became Chief Minister, and Egyptian independence was declared. Zaghlul was still in exile, and his rivals triumphant. But, of course, not for long. For he could not be kept indefinitely in exile, and whenever he returned he could always denounce Allenby's Declaration as unilateral and not binding on Egypt, and he would be right. But in addition, another feature of Allenby's policy was to consummate his triumph and lead to Allenby's resignation. When Allenby sent his scheme to London, the draft had a paragraph which said:

"As regards interval administration of Egypt, His Majesty's Government will view with favour the creation of a Parliament with right to control the policy and administration of a constitutional, responsible Government."[59]

elaborated in concert with "Sarwat Pasha and his immediate adherents". See Lloyd, *op. cit.*, Vol. II, p. 56.

[57] Despatch of January 20, 1922, Lloyd, *op. cit.*, Vol. II, p. 57.

[58] A. Wavell, *Allenby in Egypt* (London, 1943), pp. 76–7.

[59] Cmd. 1592 (1922), p. 22.

The draft, as amended in London, omitted these words, and the published Declaration wisely contented itself with saying that the form of government would be left to the Egyptian people and the Sultan to determine. Allenby was committed to Tharwat, and it may be that this insistance on constitutional responsible government originated from him. Tharwat and his friends were now organized in a Liberal Constitutional Party which, in its ideas and leaders, continued the pre-war *Umma* Party—Zaghlul's former associates. They believed that the power of the monarch should be limited, and that constitutional representative government was possible in Egypt. Now Fuad did not like his powers to be limited, and put up great resistance to Tharwat and his schemes. Allenby intervened and "advised" the King "to allow himself to be guided by his Prime Minister".[60] After more than a year's delay, the King at last granted a Constitution, but he was determined to be rid of the Liberal Constitutionalists. He chose to do this by allying himself to Zaghlul. After his first exile, Zaghlul, the girondist, the jacobin even, was on very bad terms with Fuad. Now, after his second exile, he saw no objection to humouring him in his autocratic proclivities. *Wafd* and Palace now sang each other's praises. The King even took the *Wafd's* part, and in a note to Allenby, who was protesting about the assassination of Englishmen, coolly said that this was the result of not paying heed to the desires of the majority, meaning the *Wafd*.[61] The Constitution was granted, but the King had forced Tharwat to resign, and had appointed the Court Chamberlain to carry out the elections. The first elections were announced; the Palace exerted its influence in the country on behalf of the *Wafd*,[62] and Zaghlul, the hero of the people, who claimed to speak on behalf not of a party, but of the whole nation, was returned with a sweeping majority. He was now Prime Minister and master of the whole country. With this election Zaghlul inaugurated the three decades or so of parliamentary misgovernment in Egypt when, as Cromer foretold, "under the specious title of free institutions, the worst evils of personal government would reappear".[63] As for Allenby, he had not long to wait for what Lord Lloyd called "the dreadful aftermath".[64] At the end of 1924, the Sirdar, Lee Stack, was murdered in cold blood in a Cairo street, and Allenby, with trumpets and proclamations, had to demolish the basis of his lasting settlement. His brusque methods,

[60] Wavell, *op. cit.*, p. 96.　　[61] Al-'Aqqad, *op. cit.*, pp. 421-2.

[62] Haikal, *op. cit.*, Vol. I, p. 171.

[63] In his Report for 1906, Cmd. 3394 (1907), p. 7.

[64] *Op. cit.*, Vol. II, chap. VI.

successful when practised on Lloyd George, did not now please the Foreign Secretary, Sir Austen Chamberlain, who thought they were "very like the action of a little boy who puts his thumb to his nose and extends his four fingers in a vulgar expression of defiance or contempt". He sent Neville Henderson to Cairo to expostulate with him, and Allenby, taking offence, resigned in a huff.[65]

[65] Petrie, *op. cit.*, Vol. II, p. 337.

A NOTE ON "DAMASCUS, HOMS, HAMA AND ALEPPO"

By Emile Marmorstein

So MUCH HAS been said about historical works influencing the course of history on so little evidence, that even a suspicion of an instance of such influence is exciting. The exploitation of historical analogies for the encouragement of adherents of romantic movements is, of course, very common; but an instance of a man of affairs incorporating a passage from a historical work into the substance of his negotiations is extremely rare. My suggestion is that a famous clause in Sir Henry MacMahon's second note (Cairo, October 24, 1915) to the Sharif Husain—

> "The districts of Mersin and Alexandretta, and portions of Syria lying to the West of the districts of Damascus, Homs, Hama, and Aleppo, cannot be said to be purely Arab, and must on that account be excepted from the proposed delimitation"—

constitutes one of these rare instances and, also, that an effort to trace it to its source might throw light on the meaning originally underlying it.

This clause has raised so many questions that one can be pardoned for wondering why the territory to be excluded had to be defined in such debatable terms. Not that this informal exchange of letters is to be regarded as a treaty calling for exact definitions but, nevertheless, the other territories to be excluded from the Sharif's proposed state were less ambiguously described. For one thing, if the basis of exclusion of any area had really depended on its non-Arab character, the district of Aleppo was at that time surely less Arab in character than many of the areas to the west of it; and, for another, if, as Zionist writers have claimed, the intention of the passage was to exclude Palestine (e.g. "This awkward phraseology simply means Palestine, a word that the experts could not use, because it always suffered from an unfortunate geographical inexactitude")[1], the substitution of a formula of this kind

[1] Barbara W. Tuchman, *Bible and Sword. England and Palestine from the Bronze Age to Balfour* (New York, 1946), p. 209.

for the least accurate of geographical expressions can hardly be considered to have been an improvement. All the interpretations that have so far been offered were obviously aimed at securing political advantages and throw not a spark of light on the reasons why these terms were used nor on their meaning for those who first employed them.

My answer to these questions rests on the attribution of responsibility for the wording to Sir Mark Sykes and on the validity of the *isnad* connecting him with it. The first link in the chain is 'Izz al-Din Abu'l-Hasan 'Ali ibn Muhammad ibn al-Athir (A.D. 1160–1234). His great historical work, *Al-Kamil fi'l-ta'rikh*, contains an account of the triumphs of the Crusaders over the Muslims in Syria. On his authority, the French orientalist, Joseph de Guignes (1721–1800), wrote in his monumental *Histoire Générale des Huns* that in the year A.D. 1127

"il ne restoit plus dans la Syrie aux Musulmans qu'Alep, Hemesse, Hama et Damas".[2]

Quoting him, his contemporary, Gibbon (1737–94), varied the order slightly—neither he nor de Guignes seem to have been concerned with geographical order—to the effect that

"the four cities of Hems, Hamah, Damascus and Aleppo were the only relics of the Mohammedan conquests in Syria".[3]

The next and final link in the *isnad* is to be found in *The Caliph's Last Heritage* by Sir Mark Sykes. It was published in 1915, and, according to the preface, must have been completed shortly before the outbreak of war. The influence of both Gibbon and de Guignes on the historical part of this book is far greater than the few quotations from them in it would indicate. They provided, in fact, the framework for Sir Mark's account of the period between the conquests of Alexander the Great and the capture of Baghdad by Sulaiman the Magnificent; and, I would suggest, their treatment of the victories of the Crusaders prompted him to compose the following passage:

"With the conquest of Jerusalem began the strangest interlude in the history of our modern map of Turkey-in-Asia. Islam was rolled back, the whole of the Mediterranean littoral became Christian

[2] Paris, 1756, Vol. II, Part II, p. 151.
[3] E. Gibbon, *The Decline and Fall of the Roman Empire*. Everyman's Library edition (London, 1954), Vol. VI, chap. LVIII, p. 87.

once more. Egypt alone survived unconquered. The Cross was carried as far east as the Syrian desert in the south, as far as Edessa in the north; while the whole of the western end of the Asia Minor peninsula was freed from Moslem dominion. But here again geography dictated the limits of the time and space which this new rule should endure; because the Moslems lost command of the sea the Crusades were possible, but a power solely based on sea command cannot penetrate far into a continent where the valleys run parallel to the littoral. The Crusaders held the coast but never established themselves in the strategic centre of what should have been their Empire. Had the Crusaders and Greeks united, the Seljuks would have been driven into Persia, and Christendom would have regained all that which had been lost, not for a brief period, but for all time."[4]

The whole tone of Sir Mark's chapter on the Crusades amply supports the conjecture that his emotional commitment to their memory prompted him to dictate the restoration to the Muslims of the territory held by them at the height of Crusading power and no more, and, in addition, to seek to guarantee that the errors of disunity that had brought about the final withdrawal of the western invaders in the past would not be repeated. Such motives are in harmony with the longing for continuity that distinguishes Sir Mark's social atmosphere from that of his successors in prestige and influence, with their zest for fashion and innovation.

That Sir Mark was personally engaged in persuading Arabs to accept the limitation of their authority in Syria to the areas in Muslim hands in A.D. 1127 is abundantly clear from the recorded experience of Muhammad Sharif al-Faruqi. In a letter (27th Muharram 1334—6th December, 1915) in which he introduces himself to the Sharif Husain and describes his interviews in Cairo with British officials who explained to him the content of Sir Henry MacMahon's second note, he writes:

"After they had acquainted me with this proposal, they asked me my personal opinion and I answered them in a personal capacity in accordance with my previous knowledge and the discussions which had taken place between me and Yasin Bey and some colleagues, to the effect that it was impossible under any circumstance to abandon a span of soil in Syria and that I was unaware of a non-Arab country west of the Damascus-Aleppo line as they claimed. . . .

[4] Sir Mark Sykes, *The Caliph's Last Heritage* (London, 1915), p. 26.

"This conversation took place with men of authority here and I also spoke on this subject to one of their Deputies entrusted by their government with the Arab question and called Sir Mark Sykes. . . ."[5]

At a later date, al-Faruqi would appear to have been converted—perhaps by Sir Mark's fervour—to the view that "the occupation by France of purely Arab districts of Aleppo, Hama, Homs and Damascus would be opposed by Arabs with force of arms, but with this exception . . . they would accept some modification of the northwestern boundaries proposed by the Sharif of Mecca".[6]

Sir Shane Leslie's biography of Sir Mark Sykes provides a little more circumstantial evidence. In his schooldays, he had founded a periodical called "The Snarl" which "was apparently written entirely by Mark. . . . Parodies of Gibbon and the Thousand and One Nights filled up space".[7] That he enjoyed drafting historic declarations emerges from his authorship of General Maude's proclamation on the entry of British troops into Baghdad.[8] There is abundant testimony to the prominence of his role in the whole affair. According to General MacDonogh, Sir Mark had impressed "the Arab idea" on Kitchener[9] on whose instructions he left England for Sofia, Salonika and Cairo on 1st June, 1915: Ormsby-Gore described Sir Mark as "the chief motive force behind the British Government's Near Eastern Policy in the War"[10]: Hogarth stated that "Mark Sykes used to appear, half expected and almost out of the blue" with "a not always palatable instruction from London"; and Sir Gilbert Clayton mentioned his first meeting with him "in the early days of the negotiations with the Arabs".[11] In view of his powerful position and of his obvious passions for drafting and historical tradition, could Sir Mark conceivably have abstained from literary intervention in such a dignified correspondence with the heir to a lost dynasty in connexion with a policy on which he had set his warm

[5] Muhammad Tahir al-Umari al-Mausili, *Tarikh muqaddarat al-'Iraq al-siyasiyah* (Baghdad, 1924–5), Vol. I, pp. 222, 223.

[6] Quoted from the Yale Papers by Elie Kedourie, *England and the Middle East* (London, 1956), p. 37. Mr Kedourie, to whom I first outlined my suggestion and who was kind enough to encourage me to write it down, has given me the following piece of additional information: "In a fuller version of the Foreign Office report, 'British Commitments to King Hussein', cited in my *England and the Middle East*, pp. 37 ff. and *passim*, and available at the Hoover Institution, Stanford University, which I was able to consult through the kindness of Mr Nicholas Heer and Mr Howard Koch, it is specifically stated that the idea of Damascus-Homs-Hama-Aleppo did not originate with al-Faruqi."

[7] Shane Leslie, *Mark Sykes, his Life and Letters* (London, 1923), p. 46.

[8] *Ibid.*, p. 260.   [9] *Ibid.*, p. 283.   [10] *Ibid.*, p. 288.   [11] *Ibid.*, p. 287.

heart? The clause referring to "the districts of Damascus, Homs, Hama, and Aleppo" not only points to the probability that he did intervene but also suggests his unwillingness to agree that any portion of Syria held by the Crusaders in their hour of triumph could correctly be described as "purely Arab". When students of the past are empowered to tackle present problems, they are often tempted to insist on the permanent relevance of those aspects of their favourite periods of study that particularly appeal to them. In circumstances of world war that favour drastic rearrangement of the frontiers of principalities and the rise and fall of their rulers, the temptation becomes almost irresistible.

Finally, Sir Mark's responsibility for the clause in question is indicated by process of elimination. Both the French and the Arab negotiators are cleared by their early objections to the clause on the grounds that it failed to satisfy their aspirations. Of the British negotiators, only Sir Mark was sufficiently independent of routine and preoccupied with historical analogies to insist on a vague archaism flavoured by the romance of the Crusades in preference to the demarcation lines of Ottoman administrative districts that would automatically have commended themselves to the minds of cautious and experienced officials.

© EMILE MARMORSTEIN 1961

AUTHORS OF PAPERS

ELIZABETH MONROE is a Fellow of St Anne's College, Oxford, and is associated with the Middle Eastern research group at St Antony's. During the second World War she was director of the Middle East Division of the Ministry of Information, and from 1945 to 1958 was Middle East correspondent of *The Economist*. She is the author of *The Mediterranean in Politics* and part-author (with A. H. M. Jones) of *A History of Ethiopia*.

WILLIAM R. POLK is Assistant Professor of Semitic Languages and History at the Centre for Middle Eastern Studies of Harvard University. As a Rockefeller Foundation Fellow, he studied at Oxford before returning to Harvard where he took his doctorate. He is part-author of *Backdrop to Tragedy: The Struggle for Palestine*, and author of *The History of Lebanon, 1790–1840*, to be published shortly.

ALLAN CUNNINGHAM is Lecturer in Modern History in the University of London. He studied history, particularly diplomatic history, at the Universities of Durham and London. His main field of research is the growth of British interest in the Ottoman Empire and the development of the idea of the integrity of the Empire as a principle of British foreign policy. He is at present engaged on a book to be called *The Genesis of the Eastern Question: A Study in British Foreign Policy*, and is also editing *The Early Correspondence of Richard Wood*.

ANDRÉ RAYMOND is *Maître de Conférences* of Arabic language and civilization at the University of Bordeaux. He was formerly a Senior Scholar of St Antony's and Professor at the Institut des Hautes Etudes de Tunis. He obtained a D.Phil. at Oxford for a thesis on British policy towards Tunis, 1830–1881, and is at present engaged on research into the history of Tunisia in the nineteenth century, and the craft-guilds in Cairo in the eighteenth century.

ELIE KEDOURIE is Lecturer in Politics and Public Administration at the London School of Economics and was formerly Senior Scholar of St Antony's. During the academic year 1960–1 he is Visiting Professor of Politics at Princeton University. He is the author of *England*

and the Middle East, The Destruction of the Ottoman Empire, 1914–1921, and *Nationalism.*

EMILE MARMORSTEIN was Headmaster of the Shamash Secondary School, Baghdad, 1936–1939. During the last twelve years he has contributed articles to various periodicals on matters connected with the sociology of religion. He is at present engaged on a study of Western influences on the traditional Jewish society.